KNOW AND GROW THE VALUE OF YOUR BUSINESS

AN OWNER'S GUIDE TO RETIRING RICH

Tim McDaniel

Apress®

Know and Grow the Value of Your Business: An Owner's Guide to Retiring Rich

ISBN-13 (pbk): 978-1-4302-4785-2

ISBN-13 (electronic): 978-1-4302-4786-9

Trademarked names, logos, and images may appear in this book. Rather than use a trademark symbol with every occurrence of a trademarked name, logo, or image we use the names, logos, and images only in an editorial fashion and to the benefit of the trademark owner, with no intention of infringement of the trademark.

The use in this publication of trade names, trademarks, service marks, and similar terms, even if they are not identified as such, is not to be taken as an expression of opinion as to whether or not they are subject to proprietary rights.

While the advice and information in this book are believed to be true and accurate at the date of publication, neither the authors nor the editors nor the publisher can accept any legal responsibility for any errors or omissions that may be made. The publisher makes no warranty, express or implied, with respect to the material contained herein.

President and Publisher: Paul Manning
Acquisitions Editor: Jeff Olson
Editorial Board: Steve Anglin, Mark Beckner, Ewan Buckingham, Gary Cornell,
    Louise Corrigan, Morgan Ertel, Jonathan Gennick, Jonathan Hassell,
    Robert Hutchinson, Michelle Lowman, James Markham, Matthew Moodie,
    Jeff Olson, Jeffrey Pepper, Douglas Pundick, Ben Renow-Clarke, Dominic Shakeshaft,
    Gwenan Spearing, Matt Wade, Tom Welsh
Coordinating Editor: Rita Fernando
Copy Editor: Jennifer Sharpe
Compositor: SPi Global
Indexer: SPi Global
Cover Designer: Anna Ishchenko

Distributed to the book trade worldwide by Springer Science+Business Media New York, 233 Spring Street, 6th Floor, New York, NY 10013. Phone 1-800-SPRINGER, fax (201) 348-4505, e-mail orders-ny@springer-sbm.com, or visit www.springeronline.com. Apress Media, LLC is a California LLC and the sole member (owner) is Springer Science + Business Media Finance Inc (SSBM Finance Inc). SSBM Finance Inc is a Delaware corporation.

For information on translations, please e-mail rights@apress.com, or visit www.apress.com.

Apress and friends of ED books may be purchased in bulk for academic, corporate, or promotional use. eBook versions and licenses are also available for most titles. For more information, reference our Special Bulk Sales–eBook Licensing web page at www.apress.com/bulk-sales.

Any source code or other supplementary materials referenced by the author in this text is available to readers at www.apress.com. For detailed information about how to locate your book's source code, go to www.apress.com/source-code/.

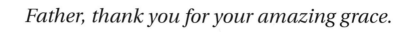

Father, thank you for your amazing grace.

Contents

Foreword

"What is my business worth?" "How do I know I am getting the right price?" "Isn't my company worth more?" "Why can't I get money for all those years I worked so hard?" "Isn't my sweat and blood worth more?"

These are only a few of the many difficult questions business owners ask when thinking about selling their "baby"—the company. Unfortunately, owners often believe the company is worth far more than the actual or true value of the company. Owners are obviously emotional when it comes to thinking about selling. It is only natural. Based on over 35 years of assisting business owners sell and buy companies, I have experienced how stressful a sale can be on the owner, and how ill-prepared many owners are as they prepare for the big event. Knowing what the buyer wants, completing a detailed exercise in due diligence, doing the groundwork . . . are all stressful. Experienced attorneys and accountants can help manage these tasks and reduce the stress. However, recognizing and accepting the actual value of the company may be the greatest stress of all—because owners believe their baby is the most attractive of all!

Luckily, Tim McDaniel, an experienced business valuator, has presented help for owners contemplating a sale. He can assist owners understand the "actual value" of the company, and provide suggestions on how to grow its value.

Whenever Tim is involved with my clients, I know they will understand the process and the valuation conclusion. I am always pleased to introduce Tim to clients because he does a great job explaining issues in plain English without complicated statistics or formulas. His perspective on valuations is much wider than mathematical formulas, high finance, or theories.

Tim's experience in the M&A transaction world is the basis of his sophisticated view. Best of all, he brings a human touch. Tim is diligent in truly understanding what clients want, and he takes a holistic approach when discussing client exit strategies.

In short, Tim has the ability to incorporate a client's personal desires with the realities of the current situation.

So often, valuations are totally incomprehensible to owners. But owners of businesses who read this book will understand fully the importance of looking at their business like an investment. They will be grateful for Tim's insight.

Beatrice E. Wolper, President
Emens & Wolper Law Firm

About the Author

Tim McDaniel is a shareholder at Rea & Associates, Inc., a large regional public accounting firm. McDaniel directs the business valuation and succession planning practice for the firm. He has over 22 years of experience and has been involved in over 2,000 valuation and planning engagements. He also provided services in the firm's former M&A transaction practice, giving him significant real-world experience to pass on to his clients. McDaniel prides himself on being able to teach business owners in everyday language how to value their most prized asset—their company. He shows them practical ways to increase the value of their business and how to successfully exit their business on their terms.

He is a certified public accountant and the author of nearly 20 articles in publications like *CPA Voice, American Venture Magazine*, and *Valuation Strategies*. He has obtained the top three professional valuation credentials (ASA, CBA, ABV). He is also an active speaker on valuation, exit strategies, and succession planning, and he has served an expert witness in over two dozen cases.

McDaniel lives in Westerville, Ohio with his wife, April, and his three children, Drew, Elle, and Charlie.

Acknowledgments

I was hesitant to write this book when I was contacted by Jeff Olson in May of 2012. For many reasons, it did not appear to be the right time in my life to devote the time needed to write such a book. However, with the encouragement and support of my family, my Rea Partners, and the Apress team I decided to move forward and those are the people that I would like to thank. I have such a passion to teach business owners about the valuation of their business, how to make it more valuable, and which exit strategies to pursue. I am grateful for those that made it possible to express this passion in this book.

This book would not exist without Jeff Olson and the Apress team. I am grateful for Jeff's confidence in me and his support throughout the process. There are many others from Apress, including Rita Fernando, who have been invaluable to work with. Because of their input and advice this book is much more valuable to the reader.

I would like to thank my colleagues and partners at Rea & Associates, Inc. I am very fortunate to be working with a group of men and women who are bright and compassionate people. This book would not be possible without their support over the years. A special thanks to my decade-long valuation team members, Bruce Bernard and Holly Taylor, for teaching me so much.

Most importantly, I would like to thank my wife and children. Without their patience and willingness to sacrifice, this book would still be a dream. To Drew, Elle, and Charlie, thank you for teaching me so much about life and being such special kids. To my wife April, I am grateful for your endurance with this project (and me) and your willingness to discuss and edit the work of a CPA. You all are such a blessing to me, and I am a very lucky man to have each one of you in my life.

Introduction

About the time I completed my 1,000th business valuation, I started to notice two disturbing trends with my clients. The first was a major disconnect between the actual business value and the owner's perception of that value. The second trend was that in most situations, the business owner's largest financial asset was the company, but they did not view it as an actual asset or investment. My clients were spending a considerable amount of time and money with their investment advisor growing their stock and bond portfolios, while putting no effort into knowing and growing the value of their largest asset—their business.

About the same time, I read some articles by Chris Mercer, the CEO of Mercer Capital, discussing the concept that business owners should treat their companies like an investment. His writings crystallized my ideas about this topic, and his influence on my thoughts can be seen in Chapter 2 of this book.

Once I noticed these trends, I started to recognize the major consequences that the business owners were having in not treating their business like an investment. I was convinced that if business owners simply changed their mindset and started to treat their business like an investment, they would have a greater sense of purpose and become wealthier. This discovery started my journey of preaching to all business owners that they need to treat their business as an investment. I am grateful for the opportunity to share my passion for the investment mindset in this book.

This book is written in an easy-to-read format with many real-life situations[1] so that you will be able to understand how your business is valued, be aware of ways to grow that value, and know the options available to exit your business. My ideas are intended to be understandable, straightforward, and direct. This book is not written for the professionals who serve the business owner but it is written directly to you—the business owner.

---

[1] To protect the privacy of my clients, I have blended companies and situations into composites that provide you with the realities of the situation without specific details of any engagement.

I have four simple goals for you:

- To encourage you to have an investment mindset toward your business.

- To help you fully understand the valuation process and the key components in determining the value of your business.

- To provide strategies to help you increase the value of your business and develop a plan of action to grow that value.

- To let you know all your options to exit your business and be able to select the strategy that best fits your situation.

If you can simply walk away from this book with a different view of your business and see it as your most important financial investment, then reading this book was well worth your time. If, after reading the book, you fully understand the valuation process, know how to increase the value of your business, and understand how to select your exit strategy, then this book will be a home run for you.

I cannot guarantee that reading this book will double or triple the value of your business in five years. The business world is complex, and you obviously don't have total control of your destiny. You can take all the advice in this book and still not have things turn out the way you want. However, when you gain knowledge and take action, your chance of being successful increases.

The book is divided into three different parts. Here is a summary of each of these parts:

PART I: Treating Your Company like an Investment (Chapters 1 and 2)

In this section, I will explain why your business is every bit of an investment as stocks, bonds, and mutual funds, and how cultivating an investment mindset about your business is the key to increasing value and building wealth.

I will also show you the consequences of not knowing the actual value of your business and why it is so difficult for you, the owner, to step back from your business and treat it as an investment.

You will also learn what steps to take in order to treat your business like an investment and the importance of each of these steps.

PART II: Knowing and Growing Your Business Value (Chapters 3–6)

After reading these chapters, you should have a solid understanding of how your business is valued and the strategies you can implement to increase its value.

I will explain the difference between enterprise value, equity value, and the net proceeds that you will receive after selling your business. In addition, I will explain all the processes and procedures that a professional goes through to determine the value of your business.

Once you understand the valuation process, I will discuss the three key areas to increase your business value and then present to you a detailed example so that you can see how small changes in your operations can result in big changes in value.

Lastly, I will take you through the process of selling from the time you decide to place your business on the market to the closing of the deal. My perspective on this comes from both successful and unsuccessful deals.

PART III: Getting Out Alive: Planning Your Exit (Chapters 7–10)

In the third part of the book, I will discuss in detail the various exit strategies and how to make a decision that is best for you. I will also explain why the entire process of choosing your exit strategy and determining your ultimate succession plan is so difficult. I will stress the importance of prioritizing this process well before your desired time to leave the business.

I present many actual scenarios to assist you in determining your best exit strategy and describe the process you need to follow to make this important decision. You need to understand all of the available options and perform an analysis to determine which exit strategy best matches your personal goals. Finally, I will show you how to develop a plan of action to make sure you are able to exit on your terms.

PART IV: Appendices

The appendices will provide you with a further understanding of the valuation process and the practical tools needed for those who are either selling their business or passing it down to the next generation.

This book was not written to make you a valuation expert and some of you may want to know more about valuation theory and standards. This is why I've included the IRS Revenue Ruling 59-60 and an excerpt of the AICPA business valuation standards. 59-60 is one of the most concise and practical writings on valuation theory. If you need to have a valuation prepared for IRS purposes, the AICPA excerpt will provide you with the IRS guidelines for business valuations and a comprehensive glossary of terms. Both of these items will assist you when you read a valuation report prepared for your company.

If you are going to sell your business in the next few years, the sample due diligence request will be of great benefit to you. This will give you a heads-up of what a potential buyer may request and will also act as a checklist to make sure you have the proper documentation and items that you will need for a buyer. On the other hand, if you goal is to transfer your business to the next generation, the sample family business creed will provide you with some ideas of what philosophy and rules you may want to set for family members who will be working in the business.

Final Words

Thank you for picking up this book. I hope after reading it you will look at your business differently and that you will see it as your most important financial investment. Finally, I hope you are able to retire rich and have many healthy years to enjoy the fruits of your labor.

Treating Your Company Like an Investment

Country Club Lifestyle

Do You Know Your Value?

A sophisticated businesswoman in her sixties called me late one summer afternoon. "Mr. McDaniel, I would like you to value my company in order to complete a transaction with my nephew." We spoke further and arranged a meeting for the following week. When I arrived at her company, I noticed how nice the furnishings were. It had the appearance of a very successful company. She provided me a tour and explained how the company started, her role in the business, and other relevant facts that were needed to prepare a business valuation. She explained to me that she was selling the business to her nephew, who worked in the company. He was in his late twenties and had been in the business for about six years.

I had seen numerous engagements like this one—a client wanting to use an independent valuator to set the price between related parties. It is required by the Internal Revenue Service (IRS),[1] and it often saves some bad blood between relatives down the road.

However, I was very surprised to find out that this engagement was different. When I asked her if my services and valuation report would be used to set the purchase price, she replied, "Oh no, the price is set. We just need a valuation report in order for my nephew to obtain a bank loan." I asked, "What is the price?" She said, "$2.5 million." I continued, "How did you determine that

---

[1] Transactions between related parties need to be at "fair market value," or they may be considered a gift by the IRS and thus taxable.

price?" Without hesitation, she said, "This is the amount I need to support my country club lifestyle. I belong to an exclusive country club and if I obtained $2.5 million, I will be able to maintain my membership at this club and live the lifestyle I want." I was stunned by her answer. At that point in my career, I had been involved in more than 1,000 valuation engagements and never had a client provide an answer like that.

I proceeded with the engagement and determined that the company was worth significantly less than her expectations. It was my opinion that the company was valued at about one-third of her expectations—only $800,000. Besides the $50,000 salary that the nephew received from the company, he had no other financial resources and no bank would provide him with an $800,000 loan, let alone a $2.5 million loan.

How could this very smart businesswoman be so wrong? Why did she wait until she was in her sixties to find this out? Unfortunately, to maintain her country club lifestyle, she would have to continue working or find a fool who would grossly overpay at $2.5 million.

Her compensation from her business was $250,000, enough to provide her with the lifestyle she wanted. There was only one catch. She had to go to the office each day and work hard to make sure that her customers were happy, the employees were doing their jobs, and the bills were paid. If she would have sold her business at the true fair market value, she would have received close to $600,000 after paying taxes and transaction fees. Like most business own-ers, her business interest was about 75% of her net worth. With her spending habits, the proceeds from the sale of her business would provide her with the lifestyle she wanted for only a few years.

While no one had ever told me they arrived at a price based on the country club lifestyle they desired to have, the details here are commonplace. Business owners guess at what their business is worth (their most important asset), and they typically guess wrong. Unfortunately, their guesswork leads to unde-sirable consequences.

▨ **Note** The wealth of most business owners is tied up in the business, but the great majority have no idea what it is worth.

Based on my two decades of working with business owners, the following are some consequences that I have seen from a wrong guess of the true value of their business:

- Unable to retire at the lifestyle they expect
- Working more years than they had hoped

- Choosing the wrong time to sell their business
- Timing the transfer of stock to their children poorly
- Selecting the wrong exit strategy
- Not exiting the business on their own terms

What if the client had known that her business was only worth $800,000 when she was 55 instead of 63? She could have implemented strategies to increase the value of her business and then lived the lifestyle she wanted. Alternatively, she could have changed her lifestyle to fit the actual proceeds she would receive when she sold her business. But now, it was going to be very difficult for her to remedy the situation at age 63.

Definitions

In this book, business valuation, succession planning, exit strategies, and the concept of treating your business like an investment will be extensively discussed. The terms succession planning and exit planning are commonly used and each business writer employs different definitions. Most use succession planning and exit planning interchangeably. However, I will not be using the term exit planning. Instead, I will use the terms *exit strategies*, *succession planning*, and the *investment mindset*. It is important that you understand how each of these terms are used throughout this book.

Exit Strategies

Exit strategies are the options that business owners have when they leave the business. The strategy that is chosen could have huge implications down the road.

There are only a few exit strategies for owners to choose from. Each will provide the owners with a different level of proceeds when they leave and will require different planning and timing to implement. The major exit strategies include the following:

1. Liquidate the business.
2. Retain ownership and have others operate the business.
3. Gift the business to your children or employees.
4. Sell the business to your children or employees.
5. Sell the business to an outside investor.

We will have detailed discussions about the advantages and disadvantages of each of these strategies, how to choose the best exit strategy for your situation, and how to implement the tips and ideas offered throughout this book.

■ **Note** There are really only five exit strategies for a business owner. The sooner you know which one you'd like to pursue, the smarter you can work to maximize the value of your business.

Keep in mind that you will exit your business whether you choose an exit strategy or not. Just this past week, a friend of mine who owned a CPA firm died unexpectedly. He had no exit strategy, and I have been talking with his brother about the options available to the family. Given the circumstances, the firm will either be liquidated or sold at a diminished value. It is unfortunate that a plan was not in place before his death; his heirs would have been far better off.

Succession Planning

One measure of great business leaders is the extent to which the business thrives once they leave their position. Succession planning is the process of preparing to hand over control of your business. There is no succession plan needed if your strategy is to liquidate the business when you stop working. But if you would like the business to continue after you are gone, then succession planning is both extremely important and extremely difficult.

Succession planning takes much more effort than establishing an exit strategy. A well thought-out succession plan will take years to develop and will include the following:

- An analysis of the various exit strategies
- Retirement planning
- Estate planning
- Personal and corporate tax planning
- A determination of the value of the business
- Insurance needs analysis
- Selection and training of future business leaders
- Contingency plans
- Timeline to implement the plan

Succession planning also requires the business owner to confront personal issues that are not pleasant to deal with, such as these: Do my kids have what it takes to be successful? Can I give up control and not interfere? Will I find fulfillment and purpose in my life away from the business? Will the business survive when I am gone? Can I face my own mortality and develop an effective estate plan?

Due to the complex and sensitive issues that must be faced, succession planning is a difficult process for many business owners. Unfortunately, most decide to delay the process until they are forced to deal with it and end up with less than optimal results.

There is a statistic that is quoted often in books and articles about family businesses. It states that only 30% of family businesses make it to the second generation, and less than 10% make it to the third. This is accurate but misleading. The truth of the matter is that most business owners do not want to pass the business on to the next generation. Some business owners start a business out of a passion for a product or service while others out of necessity due to a job loss or underemployment. A few begin a business in order to retire rich and sell at a large profit.

According to the United States Census Bureau, in 2008 there were 5.93 million existing business entities in the United States.[2] Of these business entities, 89.3% had fewer than 20 employees. These are typically small service companies whose owners have no intention of passing the business down to their children. So don't let this often cited and misleading statistic discourage you from accomplishing your desired succession plan.

Succession plans are effective when business owners have a strong desire for their legacy to continue and actively lead their families and organizations through this challenging process. The success rate for business owners that want the business to go to the next generation is much higher than the often quoted statistics. There is a great amount of satisfaction that comes from transferring what you have built to others and to helping them thrive.

■ **Note**   Despite what you read, business owners who choose early on to leave the business to the next generation often succeed in passing along a valuable entity.

A key to accomplishing this goal is for the business owner to have an investment mindset.

The Investment Mindset

The majority of the net worth of most business owners is tied up in the value of their business. It is their most important investment, but it is rare that they view it this way. Among other reasons, the investment cannot be converted to cash easily, and it is difficult to value.

---

[2]United States Census Bureau, "Statistics of U.S. Businesses: 2008," www.census.gov/epcd/susb/latest/us/US--.HTM, retrieved on December 2012.

Business owners spend more time and money managing liquid assets (stocks, bonds, and mutual funds), which are easy to value and do not have the large potential for growth like their business does. They hire investment managers who assist them in managing their liquid investments and pay them a management fee based on a certain percentage of assets under management.

Typical business owners do not view their business as an "investment." It is more of a "piggy bank," "identity," or "a job." One of my goals in writing this book is to challenge the reader to have an investment mindset regarding the business.

An investment mindset is critical for business owners to accomplish their long-term succession goals and to increase the value of their business and their net worth. The investment mindset means that business owners will

- Know the true value of their business.

- Have the mindset to increase the value of their business.

- Implement actions to protect the value of their business.

- Know how to exit their business on their terms.

- Know the best timing to implement their exit strategy.

The next chapter will further explore why the investment mindset is important and how the business owner can obtain this mindset.

What Do You Want?

There are many books and consultants (including myself) that can provide you with effective tools to assist you in choosing the optimal exit strategy, create a robust succession plan, and provide you with advice on increasing the value of your business.

The problem I have with some of these books and advisors is that they never start with the most important question:

■ **What do you really want to happen?**

For example, do you want

- To ensure that the business continues under the same care and culture that you developed?

- To let your children or employees have the business even if it means that you don't get the true value of it in return?

- To sell the business for top dollar and never look back?

- To continue to dabble in the operations after you no longer own the business?

- To die at your desk and let your family liquidate the business?

There are different strategies and methods to assist you in accomplishing any of these goals. You can hire outside advisors, read books, and consult with family members. But at the end of the day, you are the only one who can answer the following question:

How do you leave the business on *your* terms?

Before starting down the path of setting your exit strategy and your succession plan, think long and hard about how you would like to exit your business.

Whatever path you choose, you need to know the true value of your largest investment (your business) and treat this investment like the important asset that it is. This rarely happens in the real world due to the consuming nature of being a business owner. Many times, it takes a major event to the business owner's personal life (divorce, heart attack, etc.) or to the business itself (poor results, death or birth of a product line, etc.) before there is any urgency to the process.

Important   Don't let a major, unexpected event like an illness dictate your exit strategy. Have a plan in place so that you are prepared if disaster happens.

The Business Owner's Dilemma

Based on the 2,000 exit strategy/valuation engagements that I have been involved with, I believe that usually 60% to 80% of a business owner's net worth is tied up in the business. As a business owner, you cannot spend this wealth and probably do not have a plan to convert it to cash. In the back of your mind, you know that you should step back from the business and actively manage your most important investment. But it is not that easy.

You have risked it all, putting your house on the line, and working 80-hour weeks to make sure the business survives. Years later, you have created a valuable business. At this point, you may not be working 80 hours a week anymore or living on a shoestring budget. But the day-to-day demands of the business are still there. Every day, you have to make sure of the following:

- Your customers are happy.

- Your employees are doing the right things.

- There is enough money in the bank to pay the bills.

- Taxes are paid.

- You have the right inventory levels.

- The receivables are being collected.

- No one is stealing from you.

- Your products maintain your high quality standards.

- You do not have Environmental Protection Agency (EPA) or workers' compensation issues.

- You can answer banker and auditor questions.

- You can cover for an employee who quits or is ill.

- You have time for your family.

The dilemma is that the demands of the daily business issues have to be dealt with, but you are not getting any younger. Time is marching on. The good news is that life is not boring, but the bad news is that the day-to-day focus keeps you from stepping back answering these important questions:

- What is my largest investment worth?

- How do I increase its value?

- How will I exit my business?

It is rare when I meet business owners with a well thought-out plan to exit their business on their own terms. This is due to two major obstacles that most business owners face. First, they work *in their business* rather than work *on their business*. Second, they focus on the *urgent* issues and not the *important* issues. Two best-selling business books have taken these obstacles head on.

Working in Your Business

The tyranny of working in the business day to day is one reason why the business owner is not proactive in managing the business like an investment.

In his best-selling business book, *The E-Myth*, Michael E. Gerber explains this phenomenon as he explores different entrepreneurial myths (HarperCollins, 1995). He states that most new businesses are started by technicians who enjoy the day-to-day operations. They focus on working in their business rather being strategic. They eventually fail because, as they grow, the business becomes more complicated and they are no longer able to effectively manage the business.

Gerber's focus is on getting business owners to "work on their business" instead of "working in their business" allows them a greater chance of succeeding. I agree with this premise and wish to expand his thoughts to not only operational issues, but to the big picture of how to exit your business on your terms.

You can only maximize the value of your business and implement a successful exit strategy by choosing to stop working in your business and start working on increasing the value it.

Note   Spend time working *on* your business as well as *in* it.

Important But Not Urgent

The 7 Habits of Highly Effective People, by Stephen R. Covey, has impacted the lives of millions (Free Press, 1989). My personal copy of this book is falling apart because I have referred to it so many times.

All of the seven habits are important to consider. But in order for you to exit your business on your terms, it is critical that you understand and embrace Habits 2 and 3.

Habit 2 is to *Begin with the End in Mind*. Covey encourages readers to examine their behavior in the context of what is really important to them. He goes into great depth about people being busy and efficient but not being effective because they fail to accomplish what is really important to them in life. He begins this chapter by having readers imagine that they are witnessing their own funeral and determining what they want others to say about their lives.

Habit 3 is to *Put First Things First*, and its chapter is subtitled, "Principles of Personal Management." The emphasis of this habit is to organize and execute around priorities determined in Habit 2. You cannot be effective with Habit 3 until you have defined what is really important to you. Without first determining what is important to you, Habit 3 has no power because you cannot separate what is important from what is not.

In the chapter on Habit 3, Covey introduces the time management matrix, which plots the concepts of urgency and importance into four quadrants.

These quadrants represent where you are spending your time. The following is my version of Covey's matrix tailored to the business owner:

	Urgent	**Not Urgent**
Important	I Pressing customer issues Production issues Key staff replacement Lawsuit	II Strategic planning Succession planning Value creation New opportunities
Not Important	III Some phone calls Most e-mails Some complaints Meetings with no impact	IV Internet surfing Expense reports Junk mail Office pools

Typical business owners spend most of their time in Quadrants I and III, the urgent categories. This is truer today than when Covey wrote his book in 1989. With the recent economic slump, we all must accomplish more with fewer resources. Also, when Covey wrote his book, e-mail and instant messaging were in their infancy. In today's world, there is now the expectation of instant answers from our e-mail culture. It is so difficult not to be driven by the concept of urgency.

No one is calling you up and demanding that you know and increase the value of your business. There isn't an urgent e-mail saying you must spend this Friday working on your exit strategies. You might get some nudges from your spouse or advisors on occasion, but it rarely rises to the urgency phase.

Note   Time spent on important but not urgent things is time well spent and is where value is created.

The only time exit strategies, succession planning, and valuation issues reach the urgent level is when a crisis happens. The following are events that cause these issues to reach the urgent level:

- The death of the business owner
- A serious illness or accident
- The divorce of the business owner
- A child quits the business out of frustration

- Lawsuits between partners or family members
- Owner burnout and depression

Unfortunately, when succession planning becomes urgent, mistakes are made, value is diminished, and relationships can suffer damage. Concentrating on Quadrant II on a consistent basis is absolutely fundamental to achieving the right plan for you and your family.

How Will It End for You?

Determining how you want to exit your business and establishing your succession plan are both important, but not urgent issues. Yet it is vital that the business owner be proactive with these important issues. In Part III, I will discuss how business owners can do this and answer these questions:

What do you really want to happen?

How do you leave the business on your terms?

In my practice, it is important for me to get a conversation going with my clients on these critical questions. That's how I help them along the way with their desired path—and how I will be helping you in this book.

Deciding on your legacy will be one of your biggest challenges. Success is very rewarding, and failure in this area can be costly.

Summary

It is critical that you actually know what your business is worth. Guessing at its value based on your personal needs will lead you down the wrong path.

It takes a great deal of planning and effort to exit your business on your own terms. You must step back from the day-to-day operations and the tyranny of the urgent and focus on creating value and planning for your exit of the business.

One way of doing this is to develop an investment mindset toward your business. With this mindset, you will have a much greatly chance of leaving your business on your terms.

The Investment Mindset

The Key to Unlocking Value

How would you like to have $23 million in the bank by investing only $1,000 a month? It can be done.

The catch is that you have to invest monthly for 30 years and the annual return on your investments needs to be at least 20%. If you are able to get this type of investment returns, you do not need to be reading this book. In fact, you should write your own!

It is amazing how small changes in the rate of return that you earn on your investments have an effect on your future net worth. This same investment of $1,000 a month for 30 years is only worth $832,000 at a 5% annual rate of return and $2,260,000 at a 10% annual rate of return. As you can see, the rate of return that you earn on your investments is a critical factor in building wealth.

The goal of all investors is simply to exit their investment with more wealth than they had when they made the original investment. This is true whether it is stocks, bonds, a savings account, or a business. The expectation of growth in their personal wealth is different for each type of investment. If you take on significant risk, for example, there is an expectation that you may earn a large return on the investment.

All investments have risk. This includes investments that are considered to be safe, such as United States Treasury Notes or certificates of deposit (CDs) at a strong bank. Investing in or starting a business is much more risky than these safe investments. It is unlikely that you will lose any of your original investment in a CD. However, you can lose your original investment, and even your house, when you start or buy a business and it fails. Therefore, the expected annual return on an investment in a business should be significantly higher than the return from a CD.

Basic Investment Principles

Let's now look at basic investment principles and how they relate to the ownership interest you have in your business.

There are a plethora of investment philosophies and advisors in the market-place. Investment advisors will tell you where to invest your money, assist you with your investment goals, and guess on where the markets are heading. If you asked 100 different advisors for investment advice, you would get 100 different answers.

However, there are some basic investment principles that are universal. Most investment advisors believe that investors should take the following steps:

- Know the value of their portfolios at all times.
- Have a plan to grow their investments.
- Protect their net worth through diversification and wise choices.
- Establish an exit strategy for their investments.
- Implement their exit strategy at the right time.

An easy summary of these basic investment principles is this—investors should know, grow, and not blow the value of their investments.

■ **Note**   Investing 101: Know, grow, and don't blow your investments.

Investors will have different goals and strategies in the various stages of their lives. Each has different personal needs and risk tolerance levels. In addition, there are so many investment choices in the marketplace; therefore, no off-the-shelf cookie cutter plan will meet the needs of any one investor. For most, investing is too complicated or frightening to do on their own. This is why most investors hire an outside investment advisor.

Investment advisors get paid one of two ways. They either earn a commis-sion from selling a product, or they charge an advisory fee. Some advisors receive payment both ways. An investment advisory fee is usually based on a small percentage (1% to 2%) of the total assets under their management. This fee not only includes payment for their investment advice, but also includes reports on the value and earnings of your investments.

Paying a fee to an effective investment advisor can be a very wise choice. Remember how we started this chapter. A very small change in the annual return rate earned will have a large impact on the future value of your investments.

▓ **Note** It is worth hiring an investment advisor if the advisor can achieve a higher return on your investments than you can on your own.

Is Your Business an Investment?

Absolutely!

You started your business with a monetary investment and a lot of hard work. The expectation is that you will earn a return on this investment. Your return will come through the distribution of profits or by having a very large salary. In addition, you hope to earn an additional return on your investment by selling your business for an amount higher than your original investment. Hopefully, a lot more!

Some entrepreneurs have become extremely wealthy by investing in a business (e.g., Steve Jobs of Apple), while others have lost their entire investment and more. Putting money, blood, sweat, and tears into a business is as much of an investment as buying stocks or mutual funds. However, most business owners do not view their business as an investment. A 2007 survey by Laird Norton Wealth Management highlights this point.

Laird Norton Wealth Management is an investment advisory firm in Seattle, Washington. Every so often, the firm publishes a comprehensive study on the state of family businesses and how prepared business owners are for their future. The most recent national survey, "Family to Family: Laird Norton Tyee Family Business Survey 2007,"[1] was based on 788 responses from business owners across the United States. More than 85% of the businesses surveyed had revenues between $5 million and $30 million, and all of these businesses had been in existence for at least five years.

---

[1]Laird Norton Tyee, "Family to Family: Laird Norton Tyee Family Business Survey 2007," http://familybusinesssurvey.com/2007/pdfs/LNT_FamilyBusinessSurvey_2007.pdf, retrieved on December 2012.

The survey included the following observations about these family businesses:

- About 60% of the majority shareholders were 55 years or older and 30.1% of them were over the age of 65.

- Only 54% had a written strategic plan outlining the direction of their company.

- Of those surveyed, 71% had no succession plan in place.

- A total of 93% of the business owners had no income diversification and were totally reliant on the business to meet their lifestyle needs.

Also, based on my own personal observations and other family business surveys, it appears that most business owners do not have a formal valuation prepared periodically to determine the value of their business.

This information indicates that most business owners are nearing retirement age and are totally dependent on the business for most of their income needs. They have no plans on how to exit their business. They do not know what their most important asset is worth and have no plans to increase its value. In other words, they do not treat their business like an investment because of these reasons:

- They do not know the value of their business.

- They do not have the mindset to grow the business value.

- They are not diversified; therefore, they are exposed to the possibility of large losses in their net worth.

- They have made no plans on how and when to exit their business.

I started this chapter by asking if you would like to have $23 million in 30 years. It's a silly question because of course you would. Your business is just like any other investment—small changes in the annual growth rate will have a large impact on your net worth over time. This table shows how the value of a business changes with different annual percentage increases in value:

Value today	$ 1,000,000	$ 1,000,000	$ 1,000,000
Annual percentage increase in value	5%	10%	20%
Value in 5 years (rounded)	$ 1,276,000	$ 1,611,000	$ 2,488,000
Value in 10 years (rounded)	$ 1,629,000	$ 2,594,000	$ 6,192,000

Your business is no different than your other investments. Small changes in the annual rate of return will have a large impact on the future value of the investment. The major difference between your business investment and your other investments is that the business is a much larger part of your overall net worth. Growth in the value of your business will have a greater impact on your net worth than the growth in your other investments. Consider this example.

April owns a business, and she has a total net worth of $5 million. Her net worth consists of the following assets:

- Value of the business: $3 million

- Marketable securities: $1 million

- Real estate and other assets: $1 million

She reads the *Wall Street Journal* on a daily basis and has quarterly meetings with her investment advisor to discuss her marketable securities portfolio. Her goal is to earn a 7% annual return on her marketable securities over the next ten years and then retire. If she achieves her goal, the securities will be worth $1.97 million. If there is no growth in the value of her business and other assets, her net worth would grow to $5.97 million.

Now let's assume that she is also focused on growing the value of her business at the same 7% rate over the next ten years. If she achieves her goal, the business will be worth $5.90 million. If both the business and marketable securities investments grow at 7% annually, her net worth would grow to be $8.87 million in ten years.

By focusing on growing her business along with the value of her securities, April's net worth will be $2.9 million higher ten years from now.

▨ **Note**   Your business is an investment. If you treat it as an investment, it will have a large impact on your future net worth.

Treating Your Business As an Investment

How can business owners treat their ownership in their business like the important investment that it is?

Let's go back and remember the basic investment fundamentals discussed earlier and apply these to a business interest. In order to treat your business like an investment, you must take the following steps:

- Know the true value of your business.

- Have the mindset to increase its value.

- Implement actions to protect the value of the business or diversify.

- Select your exit strategy.
- Know the best timing to implement your exit strategy.

▓ **Important** When business owners implement these steps, they develop an investment mindset toward their business.

Know the True Value of Your Business

We have established that your business is an investment, and that it is most likely your largest investment. In order for you to fully understand your business and know its true value, I believe you need the following three items:

- A professionally prepared business valuation
- Audited or CPA-reviewed financial statements
- A robust strategic plan

Business Valuation

Just as you receive quarterly and annual statements from your investment advisor so that you know the value of your stock portfolio, you should receive periodic reports on the value of your business. The best way of doing this is by having an annual business valuation prepared by a professional valuator.

With a well-prepared business valuation report, you will be able to track your business's investment performance over time and identify and understand the key drivers that impact the value of your business. As you learn what drives business value, you can make the necessary changes to your business that will increase its value. With periodic valuations, you will be able to measure your progress and have no surprises when it comes time to retire or sell your business.

▓ **Note** In the next chapter, you will learn more about what a business valuation is and who is qualified to prepare one. By the end of Chapter 5, you should have a solid understanding of the entire business valuation process and how to increase the value of your business.

Financial Statements

Professionally prepared financial statements will allow you to look at your financial situation through the eyes of an investor. Unless a bank requires it, business owners are not required to hire an outside accountant to provide audited or reviewed financial statements. But it is money well spent.

Here's why. Audited and reviewed financial statements will have detailed financial notes and supplemental data that will allow you to compare your business against benchmarks in your industry. This can provide you with invaluable insight into your business.

An audit provides the most assurance that your internal financial statements are accurate. A review is a step down from an audit, but it is certainly better in the eyes of an investor than internally prepared financial statements or your tax returns.

An audit or review will make your business more attractive to outside investors and potential buyers. Buying a business without audited or reviewed financial statements is much more risky. Remember, the more risky a business is, the lower the selling price. The fees paid for these services will be recouped by either a higher selling price or the higher cash flow you will achieve by better understanding your business and industry.

Strategic Planning

The strategic planning process enables the business owner to set a course of action to improve the business performance and its value.

Properly done, this process will provide you with invaluable knowledge and insight about your business, but it is a very difficult process to do yourself for two reasons. First, you don't receive the honest feedback you need from your employees to see all the issues in your business. Second, it does not get prioritized when done internally. It becomes an important but not urgent issue that keeps getting delayed. Choose instead to hire an outside facilitator to guide you through the process. This is money well spent since you have limited resources (money, time, and employees), and an outside expert can show you how best to use these limited resources.

All businesses have a strategy, but most employees do not understand what it is. An effective strategic plan will unify the employees since everyone will have a common vision and will be working together toward defined and achievable goals.

It is demoralizing to work at a place with no common vision and with employees who are at odds with one another. This is a double whammy. It is not an enjoyable place to be, and you can be sure the value of the business is declining.

Note Paying for these services will increase your expenses. However, the increase in the future value of the business should be significantly more than the total fees paid.

Having the Mindset to Increase the Business Value

Most business owners have a vague sense of the selling price for their business. It is usually in terms of the amount they believe they need to live the rest of their lives comfortably without working.

I have met very few business owners who understand the importance of setting a targeted annual growth rate for the value of their business and even fewer who take the necessary steps to meet that goal. Those who do this are much more successful in meeting their personal wealth objectives than the typical business owner.

Once the true value of your business is known, take steps to increase it. I will go further in depth about creating value in Chapter 5. For now, keep in mind that the following are the three major areas where you can focus on in order to increase business value:

- *Increase your sustainable cash flow*: Investors buy future cash flow, so any actions taken that increase the future cash flow of your business will increase its value. Investors want to buy cash flow that is sustainable and can grow in the future.

- *Lower the risk associated with your business*: A major factor in determining the price paid for a business is the required rate of return required by the buyer. The more risky the investment, the higher rate of return needed to entice a buyer. There is an inverse relationship between value and the required rate of return. Understand your risk areas and take steps to reduce them.

- *Increase the annual growth rate*: The expected growth rate of the future cash flow levels will impact the value of a business. The higher the growth rate, the higher the value of the business. You can increase the value of the business by focusing on profitable and sustainable growth.

These concepts will become clearer to you as you read on and better understand the valuation process.

■ **Important**   The desired annual growth in the value of the business should be documented in the business's strategic plan and the owner's succession plan.

Protect the Value of the Business

If the business is the largest component of your net worth, then it is critical that you avoid a major loss of value. How can your net worth be protected from a significant downturn in value of the business?

This can be done through either diversification or by being very diligent in protecting the value of the business.

Diversification

The concept of diversification is not putting all of your eggs into one basket. But what if almost all your net worth is tied up in the business? It is easy to diversify a stock portfolio but much harder to diversify a business interest. Business owners can sell a partial interest in their business and thereby reduce the percentage the value of the business has in total net worth. But it is not as easy as calling up your investment advisor and then placing a sell order.

The most likely buyers of a partial interest in a business are private equity groups (PEGs), Employee Stock Ownership Plans (ESOPs), and family members or employees of your business. The following includes brief descriptions of these potential buyers:

- *PEG:* A PEG is a firm that makes investments in privately held companies. These firms typically buy a controlling interest (more than 50% of the stock) but sometimes will buy a substantial minority position in a business. Their goal is to earn substantial returns over a stated time period. Most PEGs want to exit their investment in a five-year time frame. They are usually interested only in larger companies (revenues in excess of \$10 million) that have a good growth potential.

- *ESOP:* An ESOP is a qualified retirement plan for the employees of a company. The owner can sell his or her stock to the ESOP plan, which will provide the owner with liquidity and significant tax breaks. The tax breaks only occur when at least 30% of the stock in the business is sold. The ESOP option is available to more business owners than the PEG option. But it is not for everyone. ESOP transactions are complex and costly and usually require a bank's participation in order for owners to receive immediate payment for their stock.

- *Key employees and family members*: Selling stock to your employees and family members can be a way of diversifying. At the same time, having a "piece of the action" can be motivating to them. However, you may not end up with the same amount of proceeds that you would with a PEG or an ESOP. Employees and family members typically do not have the financial resources to "cash you out." This means that diversifying through this option can take a lot of time.

Actions to Protect Value

The option of selling a partial interest is not possible or desirable for all business owners. Just because you cannot diversify does not mean you cannot take steps to protect the value of your business and your overall net worth. What can you do to protect your net worth from a large drop in business value without diversification?

Keep in mind that the business can be negatively impacted by many factors that are out of your control. The state of the economy, government mandates and regulations, and competitor actions are examples of items that can negatively impact your business and its value.

However, there are areas that you do have control over and steps you can take to protect the value of your business. It is tragic when a business owner has developed a great business model but then sees value destroyed by not paying attention to certain areas of the business.

■ **Important** Be diligent in making sure you don't lose value from a preventable event.

Here is a partial list and brief description of some actions that you can take now to protect the value of your business:

- *Have a buy-sell agreement*: A buy-sell agreement is the "last will and testament" for your business. It directs what will happen if a shareholder dies, becomes incapacitated, retires, or is fired from the business. It is also a good idea to have a written continuity plan that states how the business will be run in your absence.

- *Key employee employment contracts*: Your business may be very dependent on a few key employees. Therefore, your business value would be greatly diminished if one of these key employees left and lured away your largest customer or a superstar employee. Employment agreements with the appropriate covenants not to compete are essential in protecting your business value.

- *Key person life insurance:* The death of a key employee could have a significant negative impact on the value of the business. The insurance proceeds from this policy can provide funds to enable the business to recover from the unexpected death of a key employee and replace the value that was lost.

- *Compliance with government regulators:* This includes complying with the IRS, EPA, and Equal Opportunity Employment practices and meeting governmental worker safety standards. A serious violation with any of these could cost your business hundreds of thousands of dollars and perhaps your entire business.

- *Proper internal controls to prevent theft:* Each year, I hear about a trusted employee who stole hundreds of thousands of dollars. Recently, a client shared with me how a major theft had been discovered by accident. His payroll clerk got into a serious auto accident on payday. She tried to escape from the ambulance because she had placed a friend who did not work for the business on the payroll (a ghost employee). The owner figured it out when he had to hand out the paychecks due to her accident. It is important that you have in place the proper internal controls and be insured against theft.

- *Effective corporate governance:* Having an outside board of directors and/or an advisory board will provide you with an important sounding board. When the right people are chosen, they can provide you with solid business advice and help you avoid a major loss in value. Many business owners regret making major decisions without some additional advice and oversight.

- *Intellectual property protection:* Products and ideas that are unique and provide you with a competitive advantage should be protected from outsiders through patents, trademarks, and other means. An idea stolen that is not protected can cause serious damage to your business.

- *Proper insurance coverage:* A major lawsuit, accident, or natural disaster without proper insurance can bankrupt you. It is critical that you sit down with a competent insurance agent to make sure you are protected from events that can diminish your value.

■ **Tip** On an annual basis, meet with your banker, insurance agent, and accountant to discuss potential areas of exposure for your business.

Select Your Exit Strategy

It's never too soon to start planning your exit strategy. You will eventually leave your business, and it's better to do so before a life-changing event forces you out. The sooner you plan, the more options you will have.

There is no "one-size-fits-all" way of determining your best exit strategy. Part III of this book is devoted to developing your exit strategy. For now, I will introduce five major steps in determining your exit strategy:

- Learn about all the exit options that are available.

- Perform an analysis that calculates the expected proceeds from each of your potential exit options.

- Eliminate some options if the analysis shows that they do not fit into your retirement and financial plans.

- Have an honest dialog among stakeholders (family members, key employees, and advisors) about the exit options you are considering.

- Integrate your desires with those of the other stakeholders to determine the proper exit strategy for you.

When to Exit the Business

The timing of the exit from your business is one of the most important decisions you will ever make. This decision should be based on your personal economic needs, enjoyment of and capacity to work, market conditions, and your family situation. How to determine the exit strategy that works for you will be discussed in Chapter 9.

There are periods in the economic cycle when the price that you can obtain for your business does not match its actual value. It works both ways. During the past great recession, businesses were being sold at prices much less than actual value. People were scared, and banks were not lending. Only a few deals were consummated and most of these were at a price lower than the actual value of the business. The opposite can also happen when there is a bubble in the economy or in an industry.

In the fall of 1999, one of my technology clients had a $5 million offer from a synergistic buyer. The owner was torn on whether to accept the offer or not. Maybe he could get more! After all, the stock market was reaching new highs on a daily basis. I was in disbelief that anyone would offer that price to him. But in 1999, it was crazy and I was having a hard time believing any value in the technology segment. I was also starting to doubt my ability to value technology companies.

Then the "dot-com" bubble burst. The NASDAQ went from 5,132 in March of 2000 to about half of that within a year. The buyer withdrew the $5 million offer in the middle of the meltdown, and the client continued the process of selling his business. His next best offer was less than $1 million. To this date, the owner has still not sold his business.

■ **Tip**   If your exit strategy is to sell your business, take advantage of offers that are significantly higher than your actual value. The market—and buyer habits—change quickly.

Do You Have the Investment Mindset?

Do you have the investment mindset when it comes to your ownership in your business? Here is a test for you. If you answer "yes" to all the following questions, you do indeed have the investment mindset:

- Do you have a recent business valuation prepared by a qualified business appraiser?

- Do you have goal for what your business will be worth a year from now? How about in five years?

- Do you know what the annual rate of return is on your investment in the business? How does this compare to other investment possibilities?

- Have you developed specific strategies to increase the value of your business?

- Do you know how much of your net worth is tied up in your business ownership interest?

- Do you know what percentage of your annual income comes from outside the business?

- Do you know the how and when you will exit your business?

Summary

Your business is as every bit of an investment as stocks, bonds, and mutual funds. Treating your business like an investment (cultivating the investment mindset) is the key to increasing value and building wealth.

Wise business owners know what their business is worth, have a plan to increase its value, and are diligent in protecting its value. They understand the exit options available to them and develop an exit strategy that will allow them to exit the business on their own terms.

It is now time to learn about the business valuation process in plain English.

Knowing and Growing Your Business Value

Valuation Fundamentals

Valuation in Plain English

"I don't want to pay that much for a valuation," the caller said. "Can't you just put my numbers into the computer and spit out my value? I just want something quick and dirty." This is an all-too-common conversation that I have with potential clients. The truth is, there's no such thing as a quick valuation, and there's no (reputable) computer program that can provide an accurate valuation based on a bunch of numbers you input.

In this chapter, I will explain the entire valuation process by using everyday language. So if you are a valuation professional, please forgive me for not using the specific nomenclature that you are used to.

Let's look at an example that shows why a good valuation depends on much more than looking at only financial records. There is a national parts distributor that buys products directly from manufacturers and then processes and repackages the products and delivers them to the retailer. The retailer then sells the products to the consumer. Historically, the distributor's revenues have been over $100 million and the annual profits have been consistently over $4 million.

How much is this business worth? Should it be based on a percentage of revenues? How about a multiple of earnings?

The actual value of this business is less than $1 million. How can this be? Based on historical earnings, you would earn the purchase price in three months. What a bargain! Interested?

The rest of the story is that the distributor is very dependent on one customer. That customer accounts for over $90 million (or 90%) of the $100 million in annual sales. They recently lost the customer and may liquidate the business rather than try to rebuild it. After selling the company's assets and paying off all the company's obligations, the owner believes that he will be able to put just less than $1 million into his pocket. This process will take a couple of years.

Would you get the right answers if you simply put numbers into a spreadsheet and based the value on historical earnings? Absolutely not! Why? It's because of the following point:

■ **Important**   Valuation is a prophecy of the future based on the information that the valuator has as of the valuation date.

If someone has prepared a valuation for you by using a canned valuation software program without interviewing you and without understanding your business and industry, please take the valuation report and throw it in the trash. It's not worth your time.

The valuation process is a mystery for most business owners. Web sites, articles, and books like this one can shed light on the mechanics of placing a value on a business and will provide you with some education on how to value a business. However, the terms used in many of these resources makes the valuation process seem more complex than it actually is.

Some business owners will hear stories from their friends or read articles about how much money others have received from selling their business. "It was simple," says the friend. "They gave me five times earnings." This makes the valuation process seem easy.

The reality is that the valuation process is much more involved than multiplying an earnings number by a multiplier, but it is not so complex that you cannot understand it.

Hopefully after reading this chapter, you will have a basic understanding of the valuation process and be able to explain to your spouse in plain English this process. You will also know the difference between *enterprise value*, *equity value*, and the *net proceeds* that you receive after you sell your business. The discussion is still more of an overview, but a necessary one. In the next chapter, we will dive in deeper and provide more of a "how the sausage is made" explanation of the valuation process.

What Is a Business Valuation?

A business valuation is a process and a set of procedures used to estimate the value of an owner's interest in a business. The key words in this definition are process, procedures, and estimate.

A long-standing resource that describes business valuation and the important factors in the valuation process is IRS Revenue Ruling 59-60 (usually known as 59-60). When it was introduced in 1959, 59-60 was the most important resource in determining how to value a business. It has stood the test of time and continues to provide a guide to business valuators on how to prepare a valuation for the IRS and for other purposes. Because 59-60 provides the reader with a comprehensive summary of the valuation process, I have included it in its entirety in Appendix A. The following is a key excerpt from 59-60:

> *Valuation of securities is, in essence, a prophecy as to the future and must be based on facts available at the required date of appraisal.*

Let's break down this definition further. Valuation is an *estimate* of value. Of the 2,000+ valuation engagements that I have been involved in, there have been only a handful of times that an actual sale of the appraised business occurred within a few months of the valuation date. Almost 100% of the time, I had no verification of how close my estimate of value would be to reality. In part, that's because many are done for estate planning purposes, divorces, and other efforts that do not involve the sale of the business.

I'll be the first to say that valuations are subjective. The IRS concurs, to a degree. The opening paragraph of 59-60 states the following:

> *In valuing the stock of closely held corporations, or the stock of corporations where market quotations are not available, all other available financial data, as well as all relevant factors affecting the fair market value must be considered for estate tax and gift tax purposes. No general formula may be given that is applicable to the many different valuation situations arising in the valuation of such stock. However, the general approach, methods, and factors which must be considered in valuing such securities are outlined.*

How do you know if the conclusion is correct? Unfortunately, you don't. And this is where the next part of the definition is important. *There are recognized processes and procedures that are standard in the business valuation industry.*

Therefore, a business valuation is much more than simply putting numbers into a spreadsheet and spitting out a number. If a valuation is an estimate based on a prophecy of the future, how is this done? With a crystal ball? Dartboard? Truthfully, these may provide you with more insight than an analysis prepared by untrained professionals using computerized software.

Before we dive into the recognized processes and procedures of a business valuation, let's discuss the business valuation profession and when a business valuation is needed.

The Valuation Profession

When you need a business valuation, where should you go? To your CPA with his latest and greatest software program to assist him? To the Internet with its cheap and fast valuations? Or what about those professionals who travel around the country leading seminars that will get you all enthused about selling your business? Of course, those "professionals" also want you to sign up for only a $55,000 business valuation to start the process.

So how do you decide who will prepare the valuation of your business?

Business valuation has become its own profession. There are four major professional organizations that provide training and accreditation to the business valuation profession. For each one, the accreditation process includes testing on valuation theory and standards, submission of work product, and an experience requirement. Some designations are harder to obtain than others (e.g., ASA); however, if someone has a designation from one of the following four organizations, you can know that the valuator understands the recognized processes and procedures used in a business valuation:

- ASA (Accredited Senior Appraiser) by the American Society of Appraisers
- ABV (Accredited in Business Valuation) by the American Institute of Certified Public Accountants.
- CVA (Certified Valuation Analyst) by the National Association of Certified Valuators and Analysts
- CBA (Certified Business Appraiser) by the Institute of Business Appraisers

A business valuation incorporates many different disciplines and requires the valuator to have a variety of skill sets. Valuators or their teams need to be familiar with the following in order to produce a credible business valuation:

- Know how to read financial statements and understand accounting theory.
- Understand how income taxes impact value.
- Know the relevant tax codes and court cases on valuation issues.
- Be able to perform robust financial analyses.
- Understand how the economy will impact a business's cash flow.

- Have a firm grasp of valuation theory and be able to apply the appropriate valuation methods.

- Be able to research complex issues.

- Know how publicly traded stocks are valued.

- Be able to communicate the results of a valuation to a business owner, a judge, or the IRS.

In addition to these skills, the valuator needs to apply "common sense" and be unbiased. At the end of the day, the valuator should step back and ask the question: "Would I buy the business at the price I valued it?" At times, it is clear to me that a valuator's conclusion is not remotely close to the actual value. This is typically due to a valuator's lack of knowledge or experience, or a decision to provide a biased opinion of value. At times, business valuators can become advocates and manipulate the results in order to please their client.

It will be difficult for you to determine the skill and the common sense of the business valuator. So how do you objectively hire the right person for you? Of course, I am biased, but I suggest that you look for the following when hiring a business valuator:

- It should be a full-time profession and not something they do occasionally to supplement their income.

- They should have at least two designations from the organizations listed previously.

- Experience is a critical factor, similar to choosing a surgeon. You don't want your company to be one of the valuator's first projects. You should select someone who has been involved with hundreds of valuation projects.

- They should be able to explain complex business issues to you in plain English. They should also be willing to sit down with you and your family members and explain how the valuation was prepared and why they chose a certain conclusion. You want someone who enjoys teaching clients about the valuation process.

- Valuators should be willing to defend their work. I have testified at trials and depositions dozens of times, and it is not easy defending your work in stressful situations. Not all valuations end up in conflicts; however, it is good to know that your valuator will not fold under pressure if the IRS or anyone else questions the valuation.

- Ask for recommendations from professionals and other business owners. Bankers, CPAs, lawyers, and other valuation professionals are good professionals to ask.

Once you select a valuator and subsequently receive your report, ask yourself these questions when reviewing the valuation:

- Did the valuator really understand the business?

- Did the valuator consider the future industry trends and how the business will perform in different economic cycles?

- Did the valuator use widely recognized valuation methods?

- Does it appear that the valuation is a prophecy of the future?

A valuation report prepared by a member of one of the organizations listed previously is required to follow certain reporting standards. In order for you to understand the reporting requirements and the terms that are required in your valuation engagement, I have included the valuation reporting requirements from the *AICPA Statement on Standards for Valuation Services No. 1* and a glossary of valuation terms (see Appendix E).

■ **Tip** This final question needs to be asked after reviewing a business valuation: *Would you buy the business at the price that the valuator concluded?* If so, the valuation is probably realistic.

When Is a Valuation Needed?

Valuations are needed in a variety of situations. If someone dies and owns stock in a company, the IRS wants to know the value to determine any estate tax owed. If a business owner is going through a divorce, the husband and wife both need to know the value in order to correctly split up the assets.

In my practice, I categorize business valuations into two different camps. The first is the "have to" valuations, and the second is the "should" valuations. The former valuations are driven by a specific event (i.e., death and divorce). The latter are valuations not driven by an event, but based on the business owner's desire to know the value of the business. Business owners may want to know the value in order to develop succession and estate plans, learn how to maximize value, make better business decisions, and prepare for future events. In another words, they want a valuation in order to treat their business like an investment.

"Have To" Valuations

The majority of my valuation practice, as well as with other valuation professionals, involves preparing "have to" valuations. In these cases, there is an event that drives the client to pick up the phone and call a valuation professional, such as the following:

- *Death of a shareholder*: When a business owner dies, there are various parties that need to know the value of the decedent's interest. If the business owner's estate is large enough, the IRS requires an estate tax return to be prepared and the estate must send it a valuation that meets the 59-60 standards. For smaller estates, the heirs, other shareholders, and probate court will want to know the value.

- *Gifts of closely held stock*: A popular exit strategy is to gift stock of a closely held business to the next generation. Again, 59-60 must be followed in order for the gift to be accepted by the IRS. If the valuation meets the IRS standards, there is a three-year time period in which the IRS can question the value. After that, the IRS cannot make adjustments. If the valuation does not follow 59-60, there is no statute of limitations and the IRS can come back 5, 10, or 20 years later and impose additional taxes and penalties on the gift.

- *Equity compensation valuations*: If a business provides an equity incentive plan to their employees (including stock options or stock bonuses), a business valuation needs to be prepared. These incentive awards are considered to be compensation to the employees and the compensation level reported to the IRS is determined by a business valuation.

- *Dispute related to valuations*: There are two types of disputes that business valuators typically get involved with: divorce and shareholder disputes. If a business interest is a marital asset, it has to be valued just like any other marital asset. It is rare when the business owner and the spouse just divide and each retain the stock in a company. Instead, once a value is determined, the business owner writes a check to the spouse for his portion of the business value and she keeps the company. Shareholder disputes are just as common as divorce valuations. If shareholders want to leave a business or are forced out, they need a valuation to determine the value of their ownership interest.

As you can imagine, these valuations can be quite adversarial. Sometimes, the parties hire one valuation professional who acts like a mediator and the valuation issue is resolved quickly. Other times, the parties hire their own valuation expert and each side "dukes it out" in court. Then a judge with no business background decides what the company should be worth.

- *ESOPs*: As explained in the prior chapter, an ESOP is a qualified retirement plan where the employees own the stock. A valuation is required when the ESOP is established and also is required on an annual basis. When the ESOP is established, a valuation is needed to determine the buy-out price paid to the shareholder selling to the ESOP. After that, there are annual ongoing valuations that set the price per share that gets allocated to the employees' individual accounts. When employees leave the company, their shares are bought out based on the annual valuation.

- *Other situations that require a business valuation*: This is not all inclusive, but these are other events that will require the business owner to obtain a business valuation: bankruptcy, converting from a C-Corporation to an S-Corporation, a charitable contribution of closely held stock, or an allocation of intangible assets after buying another business.

"Should" Valuations

Some valuations are not driven by a specific event but are important for the business owner to have. There is no court date, IRS deadline, or anything else that drives the business owner to pick up the phone and hire someone to prepare a business valuation.

These valuations are used by business owners to make important decisions about their future. We have discussed why this is important in the first two chapters of this book. The following are some specific reasons why business owners have hired us to prepare valuations that are not based on a specific event:

- Estate planning
- Succession planning
- Selecting the appropriate exit strategy
- Determining life insurance needs

- Looking for ways to increase the value of the business
- Setting a value in a buy-sell agreement
- Setting up incentive plans for management

There is another reason why we are hired for a valuation project that is in-between the "have to" and "should" valuations. This is for merger & acquisition purposes. There is no requirement that you obtain a business valuation when someone wants to buy your business. But certainly it would be wise to have a professional assist you when you are thinking about selling your most valuable asset. The same goes for buying a business. You can pay what you want. But if you are going to make a major investment, it would be wise to have a trained set of eyes providing you with advice on how much you should pay.

Now that you have an understanding of the valuation profession and when a valuation is needed, it is time to talk about the valuation engagement.

The Valuation Engagement

I am amazed at how often business owners obtain a business valuation, and it does not deliver what they need. This is due to a misunderstanding at the beginning of the process. The business owner does not understand what is being valued and the standard of value being used. Any valuation engagement should be spelled out in the beginning of the process with an engagement letter. This step ensures that the valuator and the business owner are on the same page (see example in Appendix B). These are the four major areas that should be clarified in the engagement letter:

- What is being valued
- How the value is defined (standard of value)
- The date of the valuation
- The purpose of the valuation

What Is Being Valued?

The first question a valuator should ask a business owner is, "What are we valuing?" A common response from a business owner is this: "What do you mean by what are we valuing? Just tell me what my business is worth, so I can see if I can retire."

Unfortunately, many business owners are unpleasantly surprised at the level of proceeds they receive from the sale of their business. They expect a certain amount of dollars after the sale but can receive significantly less when the deal is done, particularly if they sold their business near the appraised value. How can this be?

This is due to two factors. The first is a lack of understanding of the difference between enterprise value and equity value. The second is that the seller did not factor in the impact of income taxes and transaction costs. This is very important to understand. To make sure this is clear to you, I have added examples at the end of this chapter.

Enterprise Value vs. Equity Value

Enterprise value is simply the value of the business operations. Sometimes it is called the operating value. Enterprise value includes the company's working capital, fixed assets, goodwill, and other intangible assets. It excludes the value of assets that are not needed to operate the business (nonoperating assets) and almost all liabilities except accounts payable and accrued expenses. For example, any long-term debt with a bank is excluded when determining the enterprise value. Enterprise value is typically the selling price for the business.

The equity value is the value of the stock of a company. It is determined by adding to the enterprise value any nonoperating assets and subtracting out the obligations of the company that are not typically assumed by the buyer of the business. Equity values are often calculated in the case of divorces and for estate planning purposes. Here is the formula for determining the equity value:

Equity Value = Enterprise Value + Nonoperating Assets − Liabilities Not Assumed

Nonoperating assets are items that are owned by the business that are not necessary for the day-to-day operations. Examples of nonoperating assets include vacation homes, luxury cars, excess cash, and life insurance cash surrender value.

Typically a buyer of a business will assume a limited amount of liabilities (accounts payables and accrued expenses). After the transaction, the seller pays off the other obligations of the company, including any bank debt.

The valuator and the client need to clarify what value is needed—the equity value or the enterprise value.

Net Proceeds from a Sale of a Business

In Chapter 6, we will discuss at length the difference between an asset sale and a stock sale. There is a huge difference between the two. Under an asset sale, the proceeds received from the sale are collected through the business entity and the business is liquidated. Then the remaining proceeds are distributed to the equity owners. In a stock sale, business owners simply sell their stock and walk away. This option is much simpler and better for the seller, but a stock sale rarely occurs. For now, we will focus on what happens with an asset sale.

Under an asset sale, the proceeds from selling the business's operating assets are paid to the business entity. The amount received is reduced by transaction costs. Transaction costs include fees paid to business brokers, lawyers, and accountants. Before business owners can spend or invest the proceeds from the sale, they have to factor in the tax consequences of the transaction. The amount of the total taxes owed depends on many factors and can be up to 50% of the selling price. Tax consequences on asset and stock deals will also be explained in more detail in Chapter 6.

The final issue that should be clarified at the start of the process is what percentage of the business entity is being valued. Is it a 100% interest or something less than that? A minority interest is a stake in a company that is less than 50%. It is worth less on a per share basis than a controlling interest. This is due to the severe limitations that minority owners have. We will talk more about this in the next chapter.

How the Value Is Defined

There are a few different standards of values that are used in the valuation profession. Standard of value simply means how value is defined. It is very important that business owners understand which standard of value was used for their valuation conclusion. The valuation conclusion will not be the same for each standard of value. In this book, I will only focus on the "fair market value" and the "investment value" standard of value.

Fair market value is defined as the cash or cash equivalent price at which property would change hands between a willing buyer and a willing seller, neither being under a compulsion to buy or sell, and both having reasonable knowledge of relevant facts.

Investment value is defined as the potential value to a strategic buyer. A strategic buyer is one who can realize synergistic benefits through the combined purchasing power of the new entity and the elimination of duplicate functions or competitive factors. Investment value is typically higher than fair market value. Sometimes it is called synergistic value.

Fair market value assumes that the buyer of a business will step into your shoes and have the same opportunities and cash flow that you have. Investment value assumes that the buyer will be able to make significant changes that will positively impact future cash flow.

Fair market value is used for most of the "have to" valuations. The IRS and the court system want to know the value based on current operations and not what the value is to a larger company that can achieve synergies from the purchase of the business.

Investment value is used in situations where the business owner wants to sell the business for top dollar and is curious what a larger business that can eliminate jobs and has other synergies will pay for the business. Sometimes a buyer is just interested in seller's intellectual property (patents, software developed, etc.) and is willing to pay large dollar amounts even though the seller has not been profitable.

This is why it is important to know what standard of value is used in the valuation. Sometimes I will show the business owner the value under both the fair market value and the investment value standard. This is helpful in choosing what exit strategy makes the most sense. Some business owners want top dollar for their business and are willing to sell to a larger business, even though they know it means many jobs will be eliminated. Other business owners are willing to accept a lower selling price if they are assured that their employees will keep their jobs.

The Purpose of the Valuation

Earlier in this chapter, we discussed the reasons someone may need to have a valuation prepared. It is very important that the purpose of the valuation be clear in the beginning of the process since the standard of value used is based on the purpose of the valuation.

In addition, there are many times when someone will try to use a valuation done for one purpose for another purpose or the valuation prepared for one purpose gets used for another purpose. I hate it when I get calls from divorce attorneys saying that they have a copy of a valuation done for business planning purposes and they want to use it in a divorce case. Is the valuation conclusion the same? It depends on the standard of value used and the date of the valuation.

The Date of the Valuation

The valuation is always as of a specific date. The determination of the valuation date is very simple in the case of an estate (day of death) or gift (date of the gift) but can be much harder to determine in other cases. A divorce is an example of where the date can be confusing. Is it the date of separation? The date of the final court hearing? It is important that the date of the valuation is clearly established between the valuator and the client.

In valuation theory, events that occur after the date of the valuation should not be considered unless they are reasonably foreknown. One day can make a big difference in the valuation conclusion.

Now that you understand what needs to be clarified before starting a valuation engagement, let's discuss the relevant factors that should be considered during the valuation process.

Important Factors to Consider in a Valuation

Valuing a business is not a simple and quick process. There are many factors that need to be considered before coming to a conclusion on a company's value.

The following is an excerpt from IRS Revenue Ruling 59-60:

> *It is advisable to emphasize that in the valuation of the stock of closely held corporations or the stock of corporations where market quotations are either lacking or too scarce to be recognized, all available financial data, as well as all relevant factors affecting the fair market value, should be considered.*

What are the relevant factors? See Appendix A for a helpful description from 59-60 of these factors. The following is not an all-inclusive list of the relevant factors, but these factors are fundamental and require careful analysis in each case:

- *An in-depth understanding of the business*: Valuation analysts need to know all they can about the business and its operations. This includes knowing the strength of the management team, the products and services sold, the customers, the suppliers, and what keeps management awake at night. This is very important in determining how risky it is to buy the business and what "rate of return" the buyer requires in order to make an investment in the business.

- *Historical financial trends of the business*: Historically, has the business been growing or declining? Are the profit margins improving or deteriorating? Are the financial results consistent or unpredictable? Will these trends continue into the future?

- *Economic outlook where the business operates*: The revenue and profit of some companies are tied directly to the overall economy of where they operate (e.g., a construction-related company). The expected future operating results are tied directly to the forecast for the economy. Meanwhile, other companies are not impacted by how the overall economy is doing because they have developed products that sell in good and bad times (e.g., Apple).

- *Industry outlook:* Understanding the outlook of the specific industry where the business operates is critical in any valuation. For example, in the 1980s typewriting manufacturers may have had very good historical financial trends; however, the outlook for the industry was poor due to the acceptance of the personal computer and word processing software. Within a few years, there were no longer any manufacturers of typewriters.

- *Management's forecast of the future:* Valuation is a prophecy of the future. It is critical that the valuation analyst spend a great amount of time discussing with management their expectations for the future and understand any reasons why it may deviate from recent historical trends. The valuator needs to have a skeptical mind when dealing with management forecasts and make a judgment call whether to believe them or not. This is particularly true when management wants a certain outcome. For instance, is it a coincidence that owners talk about all the bad things happening to their business, and how the future will be much worse than the past, when they are going through a divorce?

Only after valuators believe that they have a good understanding of a business and its prospects for the future can they begin determining the value of a business.

The Three Valuation Approaches

In my profession, there are three recognized approaches in determining the value of a business. Under each approach, there are many different accepted methodologies in determining value. The three approaches to value are the income, asset, and market approach. In the next chapter, we will discuss these in more detail.

The Income Approach to Value

This is the most widely used and accepted approach in valuing a business. In the simplest terms, this approach determines the future economic benefit the buyer will obtain from buying the business and then determines the rate of return required to entice an investor to buy the business. This is similar to any other investment that you may consider investing in. Two questions need to be asked: what can I earn on the investment and how risky is that investment?

The Asset Approach to Value

This approach estimates the value of the tangible assets owned by the business (cash, receivables, inventory, and equipment) and the amount of the business's obligations (payables, payroll, taxes, and bank debt) as of the valuation date. The difference between the value of the assets and the obligations is the value under this approach. When this approach is higher than the other approaches, it means the business is worth more dead than alive and the valuator should factor in the cost to liquidate in determining the final value.

The Market Approach to Value

The most effective way to appraise your house is to find the sale price of other houses in your neighborhood that have recently sold. The market approach to value for a business is similar to what real estate appraisers do. The valuator tries to find companies that are similar to the business being valued that have sold in the marketplace or are publicly traded companies. My company subscribes to various databases that provide us with information about private company transactions. For some businesses, like a McDonald's restaurant, it is easy to find transactions and make the comparison to determine value. While for others, like a niche manufacturer, it is more difficult to find a comparable company and use the market approach.

We will discuss which approach makes the most sense in the valuation engagement in the next chapter. Many appraisers make the mistake of averaging the three approaches. This rarely is the best way to form a conclusion of value.

Valuation Definitions

At the end of the chapter, I present some very basic calculations that will enable you to understand the difference between enterprise value, equity value, and net proceeds. But first you need to understand two other concepts that will help you better understand these examples.

- *Sustainable cash flow:* This is the forecasted cash flow level that buyers expect to be able to put into their pocket on an annual basis. The sustainable cash flow is what is available after all expenses and taxes are paid and funds are retained for making investments into capital items (e.g., equipment). It is the cash produced by the business over and above what is needed to sustain operations. In other words, it is what the business owner can spend or invest.

- *EBITDA*: My friend and partner Bruce Bernard would often joke that the definition of EBITDA is "Earnings Before I Tricked a Dumb Auditor." The real definition is "Earnings Before Interest, Taxes, Depreciation, and Amortization." It is how much cash is available before paying taxes and making investments into equipment, trucks, and other capital items. The term EBITDA is widely used in the valuation profession. A popular way to determine the enterprise value is taking the company's EBITDA level and multiplying it by an EBITDA multiplier, which changes depending on the industry, risk factors, and growth rate.

Valuation in Plain English

Armed with those two definitions, let's proceed. Remember that one of the most important concepts in valuation theory is that valuation is a prophecy of the future. Prophecy of what? It is the prophecy of the economic benefit available to the business owner. In other words, it is how much they pull out of the business on an annual basis and spend or invest.

When someone buys a business, there are two main questions that need to be answered before determining what price to pay for it:

- How much cash will I put into my pocket from buying this business? (This is the sustainable cash flow.)
- How sure am I that it will go into my pocket? (This is the required rate of return related to the sustainable cash flow.)

The buyer will perform, or hire someone to perform, a detailed analysis to answer these questions.

How Much Cash Will I Put into My Pocket?

The starting point in determining the sustainable cash flow is to normalize the historical financial statements. With this step, I make adjustments for unusual or nonrecurring items that would cause any particular year not to be truly representative of the operating results. For example, a one-time settlement payment from a lawsuit of $500,000 is not a recurring item and part of normal business operations. The next chapter will include more extensive information about the normalized process.

The normalized process provides us with historical financial trends that exclude items that are not part of the normal business operations. Does the historical normalized financial statement provide us with the best indication of the future? It might. It depends on what we learn from our study of the industry and our management interviews. For example, the historical trends are of no value to us if the business lost its largest customer, one that comprised 90% of sales.

Business owners cannot increase their lifestyle—send their kids to expensive colleges, add a vacation home, etc.—based on the normalized income level. Before business owners can put cash into their pocket, they need to consider the following:

- What will be Uncle Sam's cut of the profits?

- What big items need to be purchased to sustain operations?

- How much should be set aside to fund the growth of the business?

After paying taxes and setting aside funds to make major purchases and meet working capital needs, business owners can make cash distribution and do what they want with the funds.

How Sure Am I That It Will Go into My Pocket?

After the future sustainable cash flow is determined, it is important to determine the confidence level that a buyer would have in obtaining this cash flow. If buyers are very confident that it will land in their pocket, then they are willing to pay more for the business. If they are worried that the cash flow will not be there in three years, then they will not pay as much.

Valuators go through a process to determine what the proper rate of return should be for the business they are valuing, which includes looking at the specific risks associated with the business. This process will be explained more in the next chapter, and it is just as critical as determining the future sustainable cash flow. Small differences in this rate will make a significant difference in value.

The rate of return can only be determined by fully understanding the company's risk profile and prospects for future growth. This is done by studying the industry and interviewing management. It is critical that the valuator truly understands all the risks associated with the business being valued.

The Key Valuation Concept in Plain English   How much can I put into my pocket by buying this business and how sure am I that it will go into my pocket?

Besides knowing the answers to these two questions—how much and how certain—the answer to one additional question will determine the total price a buyer will pay for the business and the total proceeds the seller will obtain. This last question to ask is this: what am I buying? The business operations only, the enterprise value? Or the stock of the company, which includes the enterprise value? The best way to understand the difference between the two is to go through an example.

Examples in Plain English

The best way to ensure that you fully understand the concepts presented in this chapter is by walking you through a simple example.

Scenario: Charlie is the 100% owner of a company that manufactures footballs, Fantastic Footballs, Inc., and he wants to sell his business. He has found a buyer and agreed to sell the business operations but not the stock of the company. The buyer and seller have agreed that the future sustainable EBITDA will be $800,000. They have agreed to use a multiplier of 5 of the estimated sustainable EBITDA to determine the enterprise value. The business owns a vacation home that is valued at $500,000, and it has a long-term bank debt of $2 million. The buyer does not want the vacation home and will not be paying off the debt at closing.

Enterprise Value Example

The enterprise value is the value of the company's operating assets (intangibles, fixed assets, and working capital). In this example, the buyer has agreed to pay 5 times EBTIDA for these operating assets. The enterprise value of the company is calculated here:

Sustainable EBITDA	$	800,000
Multiplier Applied		5.0
Enterprise Value	$	4,000,000

Since it is an asset deal, the company will obtain a check for $4 million at closing. After closing, the assets of the company will be a cash amount of $4 million and a vacation home of $500,000. The only remaining obligation is the bank debt of $2 million. What is the value of the company's equity?

100% Equity Value Example

Charlie is excited that he sold his business for a good price and is comfortable about how the new owner will operate the business. He is anxious to invest the proceeds of the sale with his investment advisor. Since he sold only the operating assets of the business, the value of Charlie's equity is determined by adding back the nonoperating assets and subtracting the value of the liabilities that are not part of the enterprise value. The equity value of the business is calculated here:

Sustainable EBITDA	$ 800,000
Multiplier Applied	5.0
Enterprise Value	4,000,000
Vacation Home	500,000
Long-term Debt	(2,000,000)
100% Equity Value	$ 2,500,000

Charlie is surprised to learn that his equity value is not the 5 times EBITDA. In his retirement calculations, he assumed that he would have $4 million before taxes. He did not realize in the beginning of the selling process that the buyer would not be paying off his long-term debt. He needs to deduct the bank debt to determine how much he would realize after the sale and after he liquidates his company. But wait, there is one more surprise. Charlie must take one more step before he can spend or invest the money from the sale of his business.

Net Proceeds Example

Charlie's retirement plan is to travel the world and spoil his grandkids. He thought that $4 million was enough to do this. Charlie's stock is valued at $2.5 million after including the vacation home and the bank debt. Is this the amount that Charlie can give his investment advisor? No, it is not. Before he is able to spend or invest his sales proceeds, he must pay the tax man and the people that helped him sell his business.

Professional fees for a business transaction can include a success fee paid to an M&A intermediary or a business broker and fees paid to lawyers and accountants. In the following example, we will assume that the professional fees associated with selling Charlie's business totaled $250,000.

Of course, you would expect that Uncle Sam wants to get a piece of the action. There are tax consequences in selling a business. The taxes paid depend on whether it is an asset sale or a stock sale and how the transaction is characterized in the purchase agreement. We will assume that the total tax paid on this transaction was $750,000. Fantastic Footballs is a C-Corporation and the tax includes a corporate tax on the sale proceeds over and above the company's asset tax basis. In addition, Charlie must pay a tax on an individual basis after he liquidates the business to get his proceeds. We will explain the tax consequences of selling a business further in Chapter 6.

Charlie's net proceeds from this deal after paying the transaction costs and the IRS are calculated here:

100% Equity Value	$ 2,500,000
Income Taxes	(750,000)
Transaction Costs	(250,000)
Net Proceeds	$ 1,500,000

Charlie is not happy. He thought he was going to walk away with $4 million, but he instead is only getting $1.5 million!

■ **Important**   It is critical that you know the difference between enterprise value, equity value, and net proceeds.

Summary

Hopefully after reading this chapter, you have a better understanding of the business valuation process. It is more complicated than simply putting numbers into a spreadsheet—but is less complicated than brain surgery.

As a business owner, it is vital that you understand the difference between enterprise value, equity value, and the net proceeds that you will receive after selling your business.

Now that you have a basic understanding on how a business is valued, let's move on to show more details about the valuation process. In the next chapter, we will explain further how your business is valued using the income, asset, and market approaches to value.

Valuation Approaches

How the Sausage Is Made

Valuations for divorce cases and shareholder disputes are the closest we get to hand-to-hand combat in the accounting profession. Two valuation experts battle on the witness stand. We fight over future cash flows and what the expected rate of return should be on the cash flows. We have reams of paper to support our positions and hope that the attorney on our side asks the right questions and that the opposing attorney asks the wrong ones. However, many times none of this matters. The ultimate decision makers are the judges who probably neither have a business background nor enjoy listening to number nerds debate high-dollar issues. Sometimes their decisions are well thought out and make sense with the facts of the case. Other times, it is clear they did not really understand valuation theory, or they may have had an alternative motive with their decision. Going to trial on valuation issues is litigation roulette because it is hard to predict where the answer will land.

I have testified over two dozen times, including in front of a sleeping, snoring judge as well as before a plaintiff and defendant making obscene gestures at each other during my testimony. What follows are two real-life combat stories that will show you some difficulties in preparing a business valuation.

Hand-to-Hand Combat

The first case is called *"a tweak here and a tweak there make a big difference."* A few years ago, I was hired to provide two valuations of a manufacturing company for a domestic case. The owner started the business before he was married; therefore, I had to value the company at the date of the marriage and at the date of the divorce. The spouse was entitled to 50% of the growth in the value of the company between those two dates. In my opinion, the growth in value between the two dates was $2 million. At the last minute, the business owner's spouse hired a valuation expert, and he had very little time to produce a report. He decided to use my reports and just slightly change my cash flow assumption and my expected rate of return on the cash flow for both valuations. By only changing two assumptions, he concluded that the growth in value between the marriage and divorce date was $6 million—a huge difference created by only a couple of tweaks of my report. We provided testimony for over a week telling the judge why the other valuator was wrong and why our analysis was superior. Afterward, we shook hands and asked each other about our families since we were friends. The judge selected an amount that was in between our conclusions.

The second case, I call *"the 30-minute clock cleaning,"* shows the difficulty of using and supporting the market approach to value. I was hired by a divorce court to provide a valuation for both parties of a small retail store. No big deal, I thought. It turned out to be a very difficult case. The husband accused the wife of fraud, and it was difficult to obtain financial data. I felt that I could not rely on the income approach since the reported financial data was suspect. However, I was able to locate many transactions of similar type stores that could be used to determine the value of the company based on reported revenues and adding an amount for unreported cash. Since the court had hired me, I had expected to walk into court and give about an hour of testimony, have everyone be impressed with my wisdom, and then thank me as I walked out of the courtroom. The husband's attorney asked the court for a 30-minute recess to examine my file. When the recess was over, he proceeded to discredit my market method in the eyes of the judge. How could I compare a retail store located in a small city in Ohio to one that was located in Albany, New York or in Cleveland, Ohio? This went on for another 30 minutes. I attempted to explain why this approach was valid, but I have to admit that he did a great job of raising serious questions about the validity of the market data with only a 30-minute review of my file.

The point of telling you about these two cases is twofold. First of all, small changes in the assumptions will make a big difference in value. Second, I believe that the income approach is superior to the market approach since it is so difficult to find comparable companies that have sold that are similar to yours. As I explained in the previous chapter, there are only three recognized approaches in determining the value of a business. Under each approach, there are several different methods that can be deployed to determine value. Both the market approach and the asset approach have their places, but in the real world, the income approach is what is used to buy and sell businesses. Therefore, we will focus on the income approach in this chapter and provide limited insight on the market and asset approaches to value.

The Income Approach to Value

This approach values your business like any other investment. When using this approach, I pretend that I am buying the business and determine how much I am willing to pay for it. This depends on my assumptions about the future cash flow and how much risk is related to that cash flow. The keys to this approach are answering the questions that were introduced in the last chapter:

- How much cash will I put into my pocket from buying this business? (This is the sustainable cash flow.)

- How sure am I that it will go into my pocket? (This is the required rate of return related to the sustainable cash flow.)

Once those questions are answered, the valuator is able to determine the enterprise value.

There are two primary methods that valuators use when applying the income approach. Sometimes both methods are used, but most of the time the valuator chooses between one of the two:

- *Single-stream capitalization method*: This method is used when the future cash flow is anticipated to be relatively stable and has a constant rate of long-term growth. The sustainable cash flow is determined and then reduced to a single unchangeable amount that is expected to continue indefinitely. The required rate of return using this method is called the capitalization rate (discount rate less a long-term sustainable growth rate). The sustainable cash flow is divided by the capitalization rate to determine the present value of the future cash flows, which is the enterprise value.

- *Discounted cash flow method*: This method is used when a company's future cash flows are not expected to be stable and cannot be reduced to a single number. This method projects the future revenues, profits, and cash flows over a number of years (projection period). Beyond a certain point of time, it is assumed that the company will continue to grow cash flow at a constant rate. A mathematical formula determines the "terminal value" of a company at the end of the projection period. This terminal value is the present value of the future cash flows after the projection period. The present value of the future cash flows from the projection period plus the terminal value equals the enterprise value.

Under each method, it is important to estimate the expected future revenues and cash flows based on fully understanding the business and its prospects for the future. This is done through financial, industry, and economic analysis and discussions with management. After performing this analysis, the valuator will decide whether to use the single-stream capitalization or discounted cash flow method. The method selected depends on whether the expected future cash flow can be reduced to a single amount. The following are situations when the discounted cash flow method is preferred over the single-stream capitalization method:

- The company's growth rate is expected to be very high, inconsistent, or negative.

- Management knows that future results will be variable due to known factors. This could include the loss of a major customer or the introduction of a new product line.

- The company will wind down operations due to a known event.

We will focus on the single-stream capitalization method in this chapter, which is much easier to understand and apply. This will allow you to understand the basic theory behind the income approach.

Let's now turn our attention to how the sustainable cash flow is determined.

How Much Cash Will I Put into My Pocket?

No matter what method is used, it is critical that the valuator understand the historical financial trends and be able to determine what the true historical earnings have been. Financial statements may not tell the real story. A business may appear to be unprofitable, but in reality is very profitable and vice versa. Business owners manage their bottom line to provide themselves with the highest after-tax proceeds. Also, certain events happen to a business that impact the reported profit levels, but they may not be recurring or normal for the business operations. It is important that the valuator normalize the historical numbers in order to understand what the true historical earnings have been.

The Normalization Process

The starting point in determining the sustainable cash flow is to normalize the historical financial statements. The normalization process restates the financial statements to exclude items that are not part of the normal business operations.

The first step in the normalization process is to summarize the historical earnings levels. I like to use EBITDA (earnings before interest, taxes, depreciation, and amortization) in my analysis. I usually summarize at least five years of the historical EBITDA amounts and also add back owner's compensation. From this amount, I make adjustments to the historical earnings to normalize the earnings and make them comparable with others in the industry. The following are adjustments that are made to normalize historical earnings:

- Extraordinary or nonrecurring income and expense items

- Expenses that are not standard in the industry

- Owner's compensation that is either higher or lower than fair market wages

- Income or expense items relating to nonoperating assets

The best way for you to understand the normalization process is to go through a scenario. We will continue with the Fantastic Footballs, Inc. scenario that was presented in Chapter 3. The following chart summarizes Fantastic Footballs' five-year revenue and EBITDA trends:

	2008	2009	2010	2011	2012
Sales	$ 6,000,000	$ 5,000,000	$ 5,500,000	$ 6,000,000	$ 6,500,000
Sales Growth %	5.0%	-16.7%	10.0%	9.1%	8.3%
Income Before Taxes	300,000	-	(100,000)	300,000	400,000
Interest Expense	100,000	90,000	80,000	90,000	100,000
Depreciation and Amortization	100,000	100,000	100,000	100,000	100,000
EBITDA	$ 500,000	$ 190,000	$ 80,000	$ 490,000	$ 600,000

The historical EBITDA has ranged from $80,000 to $600,000. Is this a true reflection of Fantastic Footballs' historical earnings?

Owner's compensation is an area where there is a great deal of discretion and differences between businesses. Business owners pay themselves differently depending on the business entity type (C-Corporation, S-Corporation, LLC, etc.), their financial needs, and the health of the business. They do not compensate themselves the same way they compensate their employees. Employees are paid based on their roles, skills, and value to the business. Properly normalizing owner's compensation is very important. Because of this, we add back owner's compensation in the analysis prior to making any normalization adjustments to isolate the owner's compensation issue. The following is the same analysis, but showing the historical EBITDA before owner's compensation (EBITDAOC):

	2008	2009	2010	2011	2012
Sales	$ 6,000,000	$ 5,000,000	$ 5,500,000	$ 6,000,000	$ 6,500,000
Sales Growth %	5.0%	-16.7%	10.0%	9.1%	8.3%
Income Before Taxes	300,000	-	(100,000)	300,000	400,000
Interest Expense	100,000	90,000	80,000	90,000	100,000
Depreciation and Amortization	100,000	100,000	100,000	100,000	100,000
EBITDA	500,000	190,000	80,000	490,000	600,000
Owner's Compensation	500,000	300,000	400,000	500,000	500,000
EBITDA and Owner's Compensation	$ 1,000,000	$ 490,000	$ 480,000	$ 990,000	$ 1,100,000

Once the EBITDAOC is determined, it is time to make the adjustments to normalize the EBITDA. Let's assume that Fantastic Footballs had a product liability suit in 2010. The cost to defend and settle the lawsuit was $250,000, and management indicated that lawsuits like this are rare. It was a one-time event that depressed the 2010 earnings, so we will add back to the EBITDA level the expenses related to this litigation. The next adjustment is for the way in which Fantastic Footballs records its inventory. The inventory is recorded by using a last-in, first-out (LIFO) method because it provides the company with a tax advantage. However, the first-in, first-out (FIFO) inventory method provides a truer picture of the actual value of the inventory and the cost of goods sold. Therefore, we will make an adjustment to convert the Fantastic Footballs' inventory from LIFO to FIFO.

The last adjustment is for owner's compensation. Charlie, the owner of Fantastic Footballs, is the CEO and receives a salary and a bonus based on the annual profits. To understand the true earnings capacity of Fantastic Footballs, we need to determine what Charlie's wages would be in the marketplace for the services he performs. This adjustment is made by understanding the number of hours that he works and services that he provides. Once we understand this, we examine various salary surveys to determine what it would cost to replace Charlie at fair market wages. The following is the normalized EBITDA calculation after making the previously mentioned adjustments:

	2008	2009	2010	2011	2012
Sales	$ 6,000,000	$ 5,000,000	$ 5,500,000	$ 6,000,000	$ 6,500,000
Sales Growth %	5.0%	-16.7%	10.0%	9.1%	8.3%
Income Before Taxes	300,000	-	(100,000)	300,000	400,000
Interest Expense	100,000	90,000	80,000	90,000	100,000
Depreciation and Amortization	100,000	100,000	100,000	100,000	100,000
EBITDA	500,000	190,000	80,000	490,000	600,000
Owner's Compensation	500,000	300,000	400,000	500,000	500,000
EBITDA and Owner's Compensation	1,000,000	490,000	480,000	990,000	1,100,000
Adjustments to Normalize EBITDA:					
Lawsuit Expense	-	-	250,000	-	-
Conversion to FIFO Inventory	50,000	(40,000)	70,000	60,000	50,000
Normalized Owner's Compensation	(300,000)	(300,000)	(300,000)	(300,000)	(300,000)
Normalized EBITDA	$ 750,000	$ 150,000	$ 500,000	$ 750,000	$ 850,000
Percentage of Sales	12.5%	3.0%	9.1%	12.5%	13.1%

You can see that there is quite a difference between the historical EBITDA and the normalized EBITDA levels. In 2010, the reported EBITDA was $80,000 and the normalized EBITDA was $500,000. That is a big difference! This is mainly due to the lawsuit expense and LIFO inventory depressing the net income and the fact that Charlie's compensation was higher than the fair market wages.

Important   It is critical that you normalize the historical earnings. You will not be able to determine the future sustainable cash flows without preparing this analysis.

Determining the Sustainable Cash Flow

Now that the historical EBITDA has been normalized, we can begin the process of determining what the sustainable cash flow level should be for Fantastic Footballs. This is a two-step process. For the single-stream capitalization method, we must decide on a single amount that will represent Fantastic Footballs' future EBITDA. It is important that a great deal of effort is placed in determining this amount since a bad assumption will lead to a wrong valuation conclusion.

The normalized EBITDA has ranged between $150,000 and $850,000 during the past five years. The five-year average is $600,000. After hitting a low in 2009, the normalized EBITDA has increased each year. What EBITDA amount should we use? The latest year results of $850,000? The five-year average of $600,000? As you will see later in this chapter, there will be a big difference in the enterprise value depending on which EBITDA level is chosen.

The EBITDA level to use is dependent on understanding the historical trends, industry forecasts, and management's plausible forecast of the future. Perhaps the recent history will continue because Fantastic Footballs recently obtained a few new large customers. Maybe industry studies have shown that football has gained in popularity and that the future is bright for football manufacturers. If our analysis led us to believe that the positive trends would continue, then our chosen sustainable EBITDA level would be based on recent history.

Alternatively, we might have learned that the football industry is cyclical and that every five years Fantastic Footballs has some good years and some bad years. Management may have told us that they do not believe that the positive trends that started in 2010 will continue into the future. If this is true, then we may choose the five-year average of $600,000 as our sustainable EBITDA level.

Once we decide on the sustainable EBITDA level, we need to determine the sustainable cash flow. Business owners cannot put the EBITDA amounts into their pockets. Before this can happen, they must do the following:

- Pay income taxes.
- Buy new equipment to sustain operations.
- Be able to fund their working capital needs.

Let's continue on with our scenario. Let's assume that we selected $800,000 as the sustainable EBITDA level. This is because management believes that the most recent trends will continue for the foreseeable future. The bad results in 2009 were impacted by the recession and the issue surrounding the lawsuit. Management believes that future results will be slightly lower than the 2012 levels due to pricing pressures from the competition. After much analysis and discussion with management, we have decided that the sustainable EBITDA level is $800,000.

In order to convert the EBITDA level to cash, we must take account of income taxes, make an allowance for future capital expenditures, and determine future working capital needs. You have to pay taxes on your profits. You also have to make capital improvements (equipment, machinery, and building improvements) and have cash available to fund your growth (working capital needs) to sustain operations. The amount needed for working capital is a function of expected growth rate and the current working capital level.

In order to convert the sustainable EBITDA level to a sustainable cash flow level for Fantastic Footballs, we made the following adjustments:

- The taxable income is equal to the EBIT (earnings before interest and taxes). For this scenario, there is no interest expense. The taxable income is EBITDA less depreciation. The corporate income tax amount is based on a tax analysis.

- We have assumed that the future capital expenditure will average $100,000 a year. This is the amount needed to buy new equipment and make building improvements on an annual basis.

- The amount of cash that is needed to be retained to fund the growth in inventory and accounts receivable is $20,000.

The calculated sustainable cash flow is as follows:

Normalized EBITDA	$	800,000
Depreciation Expense		(100,000)
Net Income Before Taxes		700,000
Corporate Income Taxes		(230,000)
Normalized Earnings After Taxes		470,000
Add Back: Depreciation		100,000
(Less): Capital Expenditures		(100,000)
(Less): Working Capital Needs		(20,000)
Future Sustainable Net Cash Flow	$	450,000

Based on this analysis, the buyer of Fantastic Footballs can expect to put $450,000 on an annual basis in his pockets. This assumes that the buyer pays fair market wages for CEO services and that there are no unusual or nonrecurring items. In other words, the $450,000 is the amount that he can do with as he wants since there is no need to retain this amount in the business. How much are investors willing to pay for a $450,000 cash flow stream? It depends on how confident they are that the $450,000 will go into their pocket.

How Sure Am I That It Will Go into My Pocket?

Now that the sustainable cash flow has been determined, it is time to develop the appropriate rate of return needed to entice a buyer to invest in Fantastic Footballs. This rate is developed by understanding Fantastic Footballs' individual risk profile and its prospects for future growth. In addition, it is important for the valuator to have a basic understanding of investment theory and the rate of returns available on alternative investments.

There are two important concepts behind the development of the required rate of return. The first is risk, and the second is the time value of money. We have previously mentioned the direct relationship between risk and the rate of return. The higher the risk associated with an investment, the higher the rate of return that is required to entice an investor. The concept of time value of money is that a dollar now is worth more than a dollar received in the future. The value of a company is the present value of the future cash flows. You must account for both risk and the time value of money when valuing a company.

There are three important terms that valuators use when determining the rate of return required by the investor in a business:

- *Discount rate*: This is the rate required by investors to entice them to invest in a particular business. It is also called the cost of equity. The discount rate incorporates both the time value of money and the risk related to the company.

- *Capitalization rate*: This is the discount rate less the long-term growth rate of the company's cash flows.

- *Weighted average cost of capital (WACC)*: This is a company's capital structure consisting of equity (investors) and debt (creditors). The enterprise value is determined based on the cash flow that is available to both equity owners and creditors. Therefore, the rate of return that is applied to the future cash flows is a blend of cost of the equity and debt.

Determining the Required Rate of Return

The first step in developing the rate of return is to determine the discount rate. This is the rate of return that an equity investor needs in order to invest in your business. There are two popular ways that valuation professionals use in determining the discount rate: the "build-up" approach and the capital asset pricing model (CAPM). The build-up approach is based on the premise that a company's discount rate is composed of a number of identifiable return factors that are added together, or "built up," into a total required rate of return. CAPM theory holds that the cost of equity is equal to the risk-free rate of return, plus a risk analysis based on similar companies that are publicly traded. The major difference between the two approaches is that the CAPM adds an analysis of public market data to the discount rate calculation. Each approach includes a risk premium component that reflects the fact that investors must be paid to take any risk above that of a "risk-free" investment. The difference between the risk-free rate of return and the total return from an equity investment is called a *risk premium*.

The rest of this section will be devoted to the build-up approach in developing a discount rate. The CAPM is too complex for the purposes of this book and usually is applied in the valuation of very large companies.

The build-up approach follows this step-by-step process:

1. First, we determine what a risk-free investment is. In the valuation profession, long-term US Treasury bonds are considered to be risk-free investments. I prefer to use the 20-year US Treasury bond rate, as of the valuation date, for my risk-free rate.

2. The next step is to add an "equity risk premium." This is the premium that equity investors received in the US public markets over and above the risk-free return. There are a couple of studies that valuators use to determine this equity risk premium. Recently, the equity risk premium has been in the 8% to 14% range. The level of the premium depends on the size of the business being valued. For companies with revenues of less than $100 million, the equity risk premium is at the high end of the range.

3. After applying an equity risk premium, we must decide whether to make an adjustment for industry risks. The risk profile for each industry is different, and the industry may be more risky or less risky than the general equity market. There is an annual published resource called *Ibbotson SBBI Valuation Yearbook* that provides industry risk profiles.

4. The final risk adjustment is called the specific company risk premium. This premium is determined by the individual characteristics of each business. Some businesses have large risk premiums while others have none or small premiums. This is one of the most subjective adjustments that valuators make and where most valuation battles are fought in conflict valuations. Some of the most popular adjustments are made for the following:

    •   Customer concentration issues

    •   Thin or inexperienced management team

    •   Reliance on one or two key employees

    •   Pending lawsuits

- Violation of governmental regulations
- Inconsistency of historical earnings
- Competitive factors
- Limited access to raw materials and employees
- Life cycle of products or services

Let's return to the Fantastic Footballs scenario. The risk-free rate is based on the 20-year US Treasury Bond rate as of the valuation date. The equity risk and industry risk premium are based on studies that we purchased from an outside source. The final step is to determine the specific company risk premium. This is solely based on the valuator's subjective analysis. For Fantastic Footballs, it is a concern that one customer accounts for 25% of the total revenues. Also, the business is dependent on Charlie's relationships with his customers and the fact that he has not developed a sales force or a second line of executives. If something happened to Charlie, the customers may go elsewhere. The following is an example of determining the discount rate by using the build-up approach:

Long-term 20 Year US Treasury Bond Rate	3.0%
Equity Risk Premium	13.0%
Industry Risk Premium	1.0%
Specific Company Risk Premium	7.0%
Discount Rate	24.0%

Once a discount rate is developed, it is important to compare it with the returns of alternative investments. The source I like best for this step is the "Pepperdine Private Capital Markets Project—Survey Report 2011–2012."[1] This survey provides the required rate of returns required by angel, venture capital, private equity and mezzanine investors. I make a comparison of my developed discount rate to the required returns of mezzanine investors and private equity groups (PEGs). Mezzanine investors provide debt (and sometimes equity) financing to businesses. The debt is usually not fully secured and is subordinate to other creditors. Per the Pepperdine survey, the typical return required by a mezzanine investor is in the 19% to 21% range. We have mentioned PEGs previously and, per the survey, the required return on their investments is in the 25% to 30% range. This survey is an excellent gauge to use as a reasonableness test of the calculated discount rate. The rate of return required for very risky investments in a business could exceed 30%.

---

[1] Pepperdine University, "Pepperdine Private Capital Markets Project—Survey Report 2011–2012," http://bschool.pepperdine.edu/appliedresearch/research/pcmsurvey/. This survey is free to anyone who requests it.

The WACC is based on the business's optimal capital structure. This is done by analyzing the debt structures of other companies in the industry and the company's debt capacity. To calculate the WACC, we multiply the returns required for each component of capital (equity and debt) by its contribution to the total capital. The debt component is the cost of debt financing for the company on an after-tax basis. This is determined by using the company's current market interest rate for debt financing and reducing that rate for the tax benefit of paying interest. For Fantastic Footballs, let's assume that capital structure should be 70% equity and 30% debt and the market interest rate for its debt financing is 6.0% with an income tax rate of 33.0%. The required equity return is 24% as developed previously and the after-tax return of debt financing is 4%. Therefore, the WACC would be calculated this way:

	Rate	Weight Applied	WACC
Equity Factor	24.0%	70.0%	16.8%
Debt Factor	4.0%	30.0%	1.2%
Weighted Average Cost of Capital			18.0%

The calculation of the capitalization rate is a very simple calculation. It is the WACC less the long-term growth rate for the business. When I say long-term, I mean forever. One of the biggest mistakes that I see in other valuation reports is that the long-term growth rate is too high. I have been able to discredit another valuator by showing the court that the business being valued will be larger than Microsoft in 30 years based on the other valuator's growth rate. The growth rate should not be significantly higher than the overall growth rate for the industry and the U.S economy. It rarely is above 4.0%. If a business expects very high growth for the next few years, the discounted cash flow method should be used.

For Fantastic Footballs, we will use a 3.0% long-term growth rate and thus, the capitalization rate is 15.0% (WACC of 18% less the 3.0% growth rate).

Calculating the Enterprise Value

In the last chapter, I mentioned that the enterprise value is the price that you can sell your business operations for. To calculate the enterprise value of Fantastic Footballs by using the income approach, we simply divide the future sustainable cash flow by the developed required rate of return. The following is the enterprise value of the company by using the assumptions developed in this chapter:

Future Sustainable Net Cash Flow	$	450,000
Required Rate of Return		15.0%
Enterprise Value	$	3,000,000

Remember the case in the beginning of this chapter—*a tweak here and a tweak there makes a big difference?* Let's make a tweak here and there and see if this is true. Let's assume that another valuator prepared a valuation of Fantastic Footballs. He disagrees with me on only two assumptions. First, he believes that the future sustainable EBITDA should be the five-year average of $600,000 and that the sustainable cash flow is $300,000. Second, he disagrees with the 15.0% required return that I developed and believes it should be 20%. These changes do not seem large, but they make a significant difference in value as shown here:

Future Sustainable Net Cash Flow	$	300,000
Required Rate of Return		20.0%
Enterprise Value	$	1,500,000

Only two changes were made in the assumptions, but they made a huge difference. The changes don't appear to be major, but the valuation change is significant. You can see why there are valuation battles in the courtroom and with the IRS. Who is right? We may never know since Fantasy Footballs, Inc. is not for sale.

The development of the sustainable cash flows and the required rate of return require many judgment calls by the valuator. Little changes mean big differences in value. This is why it is important for you to understand and be involved in the valuation process. Just as the income approach requires many subjective factors, so does the market approach.

The Market Approach to Value

You may be familiar with the market approach to value. Most of you have bought a house or have refinanced your mortgage. As part of the process, the bank requires an appraisal of your home. Appraisers locate homes in your neighborhood that have recently sold. They then compare the homes that have sold that are similar in size and location to your home. They may make some adjustments for square footage, a finished basement, and other items to the homes that have sold. With this data, appraisers make an estimate of the value of your home.

This is very effective. What better evidence of value than recent actual transactions of a similar type of investment?

Valuators attempt to do a similar process in valuing a business under the market approach. There is a search for similar types of companies (guideline companies) that have actually been sold or are publically traded. They make adjustments to the data obtained from the guideline companies. They then apply this information to the business being valued to determine a value under the market approach. However, meaningful and ample data from similar companies is a challenge to obtain. Many times, it is difficult to make the right conclusion. For this reason, I usually place less reliance on the market approach and use it to support the valuation conclusion arrived from the income approach.

The following are the two valuation methods that are used under the market approach when valuing a company:

- The Guideline Public Company Method
- The Guideline Transaction (Merger and Acquisition) Method

The Guideline Public Company Method uses the market data and share prices of publicly traded companies to derive a value. Valuators look for companies that are publicly traded and similar to the business being valued to serve as a benchmark in the valuation. Typically, I only use this method for companies with revenues in excess of $50 million. An exception is when I am valuing a community bank. There are hundreds of small community banks that are publicly traded.

This method is misapplied frequently. I have seen a valuation analyst try to use this method to value a small software company with $5 million in sales. The comparable companies used included Microsoft and Oracle, which is ridiculous. The only thing that Microsoft and a small software company have in common is that they develop and sell software. This is like comparing an NFL team to a middle school flag football team. They both play football, but that is all they have in common.

If guideline companies are located, the value of a company is based on multiples derived from publicly traded companies and ongoing earnings (e.g., net income and EBITDA).

The Guideline Transaction Method locates companies that have sold in the marketplace as a benchmark in valuing a company. This is the method that I used when the lawyer cleaned my clock after reviewing my file for 30 minutes.

Several databases are available that provide the actual sale transactions of closely held companies. These databases are populated by business brokers who self-report their transactions. For a business like McDonald's, this method can be used with confidence. Each McDonald's operates in a similar fashion, and there are a lot of transactions data to analyze. What about a football manufacturer? How about your business? How many businesses are like yours for which transaction data can be reviewed?

How do valuators prepare a market approach to value if they cannot find comparable companies or the data received is not reliable? What I do is use generic surveys (like the Pepperdine study) and other sources that provide transactional data by broad industries and size of business. The Pepperdine study provides the average EBITDA multipliers for different industries by size of business. This information comes from investment bankers and business brokers, and it is helpful in determining the reasonableness of the income approach conclusion.

In Chapter 3, we prepared a value of the enterprise value of Fantastic Footballs based on the market approach. Here is that calculation again:

Sustainable EBITDA	$ 800,000
Multiplier Applied	5.0
Enterprise Value	$ 4,000,000

There is one more approach that is used to value a business—the asset approach.

The Asset Approach to Value

This approach is effective for an asset holding company (real estate and liquid investments) and for companies that are worth more dead than alive. These companies have a significant amount of physical assets (inventory, equipment, and receivables) but minimal or no profits.

If the value under the asset approach is higher than the values calculated under the income approach and market approach, then the valuator should consider the value under an orderly liquidation. The liquidation method assumes that a company is worth more under a liquidation premise than a going-concern entity. More on the liquidation approach will be discussed in Chapter 8.

The asset approach values the individual assets and liabilities of the business. Under this approach, the fair market value of the assets less the company's total obligations is the value of the company.

This approach is usually not used in the valuation of a going concern. A company's value is determined by its ability to generate cash flow, not by the value of its assets individually. It generally carries little or no weight in comparison to the income and market approaches; therefore, we will not provide any further analysis on this approach.

Determining Equity Value

The equity value is another name for the value of the company's stock. This is what is valued and reported to the IRS when you make a gift to a child and the value that is used to divide assets in a divorce. As stated in Chapter 3, the equity value is determined by adding to the enterprise value the value of the nonoperating assets and subtracting out the obligations that are not typically assumed by a buyer of the business. Here is the formula of the equity value again:

Equity Value = Enterprise Value + Nonoperating Assets − Liabilities Not Assumed

The first step in determining the equity value is concluding what the enterprise value is. For Fantastic Footballs, Inc., we have prepared a value based on the income approach and the market approach. Let's assume under the asset approach that the value of Fantasy Footballs is $1.5 million. The following is a summary of the calculated values:

Enterprise Value	
Income Approach	$ 3,000,000
Market Approach	$ 4,000,000
Asset Approach	$ 1,500,000

What should our enterprise value conclusion be? Is it a simple average of the three approaches? Absolutely not! The asset approach should not be a factor for Fantastic Footballs since it is a going concern that has a nice profit level. Should the market approach be considered? It depends on how confident valuators feel about the comparable companies. Typically, more weight is placed on the income approach, and in this case we will conclude an enterprise value of $3.2 million.

Let's assume during our financial analysis that we discovered that Fantastic Footballs owns a large life insurance policy on Charlie. It has a death benefit of $5 million and a cash surrender value of $500,000. Tomorrow, the company could cash in the policy to the insurance company and receive $500,000. Even though the insurance policy is important, it is not necessary to operate the business. Nonoperating assets are items that are owned by the business that are not necessary for the day-to-day operations.

We will assume that Fantasy Footballs has a normal working capital level and a long-term bank note of $1.2 million. This note is a liability that would not be assumed in a typical business transaction and needs to be deducted to determine the equity value.

The following is the equity value of Fantasy Footballs with the previously mentioned assumptions:

Enterprise Value	$ 3,200,000
Cash Surrender Value Life Insurance	500,000
(Less): Interest Bearing Debt	(1,200,000)
Equity Value	$ 2,500,000

Value per Share

Our valuation conclusion usually includes a value-per-share amount. This should be a simple calculation, right? Take the equity value divided by the number of shares outstanding. Many times it is this simple, but other times it is not. If the business has stock options or other synthetic equity, additional calculations need to be made to determine the value per share.

There is a difference in the value per share between a controlling interest and one that does not have control. Why? If you own one out of 100 shares in a company, what can you do with that? Can you set your salary, declare a dividend, or force a sale of the company? The answers are no, no, and no. Only a majority shareholder can do those things. What rights does a minority shareholder have? It depends on your state and the language of your shareholder agreement (if you have one).

Because of the limitations associated with a minority interest, discounts must be applied when valuators are asked to value a minority interest. The exception is if there is an agreement that says valuators should not apply the discounts in the valuation.

There are two discounts that valuators apply to a minority interest. The first is a lack of control discount, and the second is a lack of marketability discount.

Valuators are often asked to prepare the valuation of a minority interest. Most requests are related to the gift of a company's stock from a parent to a child. We will discuss this in more detail in Chapter 8. The other situation is the exit of a shareholder from a business. This exit could be by choice or by force. Should a discount be applied in this situation? At times, there is disagreement among shareholders about whether these discounts apply. If you are a shareholder who has a minority interest, make sure that you have a buy-sell or shareholder agreement that specifies whether your interest should be reduced by the lack of control and a marketability discount.

There are many studies and court cases that can be examined to determine the appropriate discount level for a minority interest. I will not bore you with these studies or court cases. It is important for you know that the value per share for a minority interest is lower than the value per share for a controlling interest. Included next is the value-per-share calculation for Fantastic Footballs. Let's assume that there are 100 common shares outstanding and that the appropriate discount for the lack of control discount is 12% and the lack of marketability discount is 25%. The value of a minority nonmarketable common share is calculated as follows:

Controlling Interest Per Share	$	25,000
Lack of Control (Minority) Discount		(3,000)
Marketable Minority Interest	$	22,000
Lack of Marketability Discount		(5,500)
Nonmarketable Minority Interest	$	16,500

The value of minority shareholder's' share of stock is 34% less than the value of a controlling interest. In the real world of valuation, a minority interest usually has a 20% to 50% reduction in value when compared with a controlling interest. The level of the discount depends on the company's dividend policy, written shareholder agreements, and whether there will be a liquidating event in the future (sale, public offering, or liquidation).

Summary

After reading these last two chapters, I hope you have a better understanding of the entire valuation process. It is not a very clean process, but it's not as messy as making sausage.

So if you call me and ask for a formula to value your business or ask for something quick and dirty, you will understand why I will say that I am not interested in assisting you. Valuation is so much more than a formula or putting numbers in a spreadsheet. The valuator has to really understand the business in order to develop the sustainable cash flow and to develop the appropriate rate of return.

Most valuators rely heavily on the income approach to value. This approach is the same mindset that someone buying your business will have. The market approach may apply to your situation depending on whether the valuator can locate comparable companies that have sold or are publicly traded. The asset approach is rarely used for a going concern. The exception is when the business owner can achieve more proceeds by liquidating the business than through continued operations.

Now that you have a good understanding of the entire valuation process, it is time to discuss ways to make your business more valuable. In the next chapter, we will discuss the various strategies you can implement to grow the value of your business.

Growing Your Value

Becoming More Attractive

Tim is a single young man in his early 20s. He wants to get married, have three kids, and a house in the country with a couple of dogs. It's a great plan, but the only thing missing is a wife. At this point, Tim doesn't have a girlfriend or any prospects. Tim asked a couple of his good friends about the best way to find a girlfriend that could become his spouse. Should he use a dating service? Can they introduce him to someone?

Will, Tim's best friend from childhood, calls him up and says that they need to talk. Will and Tim meet up at the local pub, and Will orders a couple of stiff drinks. He looks very uncomfortable and tells Tim that he has something very personal to tell him. He says, "My friend, before you start looking for a spouse you need to make yourself more attractive. You dress like a slob and don't brush your teeth or shower. You live in your parent's basement and drive a rusted-out car without a heater or air conditioner. You don't have a job or any prospects for a good job. And finally, when you meet a girl you only talk about yourself while looking at your shoes."

After what seems like an eternity to Will, Tim responds and says, "Thank you for telling me this. It took a great deal of courage to say these things to me, and I know you said it because you care about me." Will is now more at ease, and they continue their discussion. At some point, Tim says that over the next couple of years, he is not going to look for a girlfriend but instead concentrate on making himself a better "catch." They devise a plan that starts with Tim brushing his teeth and taking a shower.

You know by now that this is not a book about dating and personal improvement. The point of this story is that before you go out and look for a possible suitor for your business, you need to make it as attractive as possible. Even if you don't intend to sell your business, it is important that you consider ways to make your business more attractive and healthy. By doing so, you will enjoy running your business, make more money, and make it easier for your kids to continue your legacy.

Having the Mindset to Increase the Business Value

It all starts with a "mindset." Do you treat your business "like an investment" or as a vehicle to support your lifestyle? Business owners who have written goals and plans to increase their value will be more successful in increasing the value of their business than those who simply hope the value will increase without having any concrete plans on how to make that happen.

Once you understand what your business is worth, the next step is to set goals on where you want the value to be in the future. How much do you want your business to increase in value one year from now? Where do you want the value to be when you exit the business? Not many business owners take the time to set specific goals for their business value as well as written strategies to achieve those goals. The few that I've witnessed doing this have been much more successful in growing the value of their business than the typical business owner.

■ **Important**   You should include your valuation goals and the strategies to achieve these goals as part of your strategic plan and succession plan.

If you have no intention of selling your business, should you set goals and develop plans to increase its value? Absolutely! Setting a course to increase your business value today will provide you with many important benefits besides a higher selling price. As introduced earlier in Chapter 2, the following are three key areas to focus on to increase your business value (Figure 5-1):

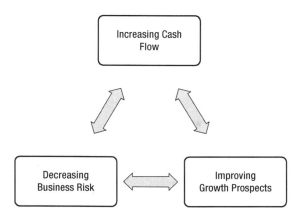

Figure 5-1. Focus on these three areas to increase your business value

How would you feel about your business if it had a better cash flow, fewer risks, and a higher growth rate? I bet it would be much easier to get out of bed in the mornings. If you can accomplish these three items, there will be a number of benefits besides a higher selling price:

- More cash available to distribute to yourself or to reinvest in your business

- Sleeping better at night with less stress and worry after reducing business risk

- A healthier business that will allow you to withstand a downturn in your industry or the economy

- Being able to react quickly to an opportunity that may present itself

- A more exciting and pleasant work atmosphere

- Increasing your retirement contributions, which will allow you to have greater flexibility in choosing your exit strategy

There are additional benefits as well, but it all starts with your decision to increase the value of your business and develop a plan to make your business more attractive to others.

If your business is the Brad Pitt or Angelina Jolie of the business world, you will have no problems obtaining suitors. You can skip the rest of this chapter. If not, please read on to learn about strategies to make your business more attractive. Besides increasing your cash flow, reducing your business risks, and developing a growth plan, it is important that your business does not have any hygiene issues that will turn off any potential buyers. Also, your business will be more attractive to suitors if it has a professional and sophisticated look to it. The remainder of this chapter is focused on making your business more valuable and attractive through the following strategies:

- Improving your business hygiene

- Increasing your sustainable cash flow

- Reducing your business risks

- Developing a growth plan

- Professionalizing your business

The best way to understand how these areas will impact your business value is to walk through a scenario. We will see how the value of Drew's business, Sensational Snacks, Inc., grows as we implement these strategies. You will be amazed by how much Drew's business increases in value without a major overhaul of the business.

Drew's Sensational Snacks

Drew is the 100% owner of Sensational Snacks, Inc., which is a manufacturer of potato chips and pretzels. The business has been in operation for 25 years, and Drew is the 60-year-old founder. He has a son and a daughter in the business and has not fully developed his exit strategy and succession plan. He wants to pass down the business to his kids, but he does not have enough money saved up to retire in the near future. Drew works 60 hours a week and is a control freak. He is the CEO and not a very good delegator. His daughter is in charge of accounting, and his son leads the purchasing department. The other members of the management team include the plant manager who has been with the business for 20 years and a sales manager who has worked for the company for 6 years. The following are some additional facts about the business:

- The business has one large customer: a supermarket chain that comprises 30% of revenues. The next two biggest customers account for 12% and 8% of revenues, respectively. Drew's top three customers are 50% of the total revenues.

- The historical sales and profit levels have been inconsistent. In the past five years, Drew had one great year, two decent years, and two bad years. His profits depend on potato prices, competitors' pricing actions, and the top three customers' buying habits.

- The average annual growth rate has been 2% over the past five years. The industry forecasts 3.5% growth over the next five years.

- Drew takes out $220,000 a year in wages and has full benefits. In addition, the business pays for all of his family vehicle expenses and an annual "business trip" for the family. These additional benefits are in the $30,000 range annually.

- Drew is unsure about his exit strategy. He would like to see the business continue in the family, but he cannot afford to gift it to his children and they don't have the resources to buy it. Also, he can't decide which child would be the best leader.

- Outside of the business, Drew has a net worth of $1.2 million, with $700,000 in liquid investments (savings, stocks, bonds, and mutual funds) and $500,000 in real estate. His investment advisor has told him that he needs $3 million in liquid investments to retire at the lifestyle he wants at age 65.

Here is a summary of last year's income statement. These results are very similar to the average of the past five years. Some years have been better, and some have been worse. Drew believes that his results over the next few years will be similar.

Revenues	$	6,000,000	100.0%
Cost of Goods Sold		4,200,000	70.0%
Gross Margin		1,800,000	30.0%
Operating Expenses		1,300,000	21.7%
Net Income Before Taxes		500,000	8.3%
Income Taxes		175,000	2.9%
Net Income	$	325,000	5.4%

Based on these facts, what is Sensational Snacks' enterprise value on a fair market basis? Can Drew sell his business and have a comfortable retirement? Remember, "fair market value" basis does not factor in any synergistic benefits. For this example, let's assume that the sustainable cash flow is similar to the after-tax net income level. Based on this fact pattern, a buyer of Sensational Snacks can expect to put $325,000 in his pockets on an annual basis.

What is the required to entice someone to make an investment in Sensational Snacks? The risk concerns that a buyer would have include the following:

- The top three customers make up 50% of the revenues and the largest customer is 30% of revenues. The loss of the largest customer would be devastating.

- The business is very dependent on Drew. If something happened to him, business operations would suffer. There is no succession plan in place, and no one is specified to be the leader after Drew leaves. Outside of his son and daughter, there are only two individuals who are part of the management team.

- The historical earnings have been inconsistent. This is due to the volatility of potato prices and the fact that, at times, large competitors deeply discount their prices, hurting Drew's sales.

Based on these three major risk factors, it is determined that a 25% rate of return is required to entice an investor. The following is the calculated enterprise value:

Sustainable Net Cash Flow	$ 325,000
Required Rate of Return	25.0%
Enterprise Value	$ 1,300,000

At this point in time, Drew could sell the business operations for $1.3 million For the purpose of this example, let's assume that Sensational Snacks does not have any nonoperating assets or any liabilities that Drew will have to pay off when the business is sold. Therefore, the equity value equals the enterprise value. Let's also assume that the tax and transaction cost related to the transaction is $400,000. Based on this fact pattern, the amount that Drew can invest or spend after the sale of his business is $900,000.

After a sale, Drew would have $1.6 million in liquid assets and $500,000 of real estate. His net worth is $2.1 million but he would no longer have his $220,000 salary and the related benefits. How long will it be before Drew runs out of money in retirement? Based on his lifestyle, he will run out of money before he turns 75. He is frustrated because he feels like he will have to work another 10 years to meet his financial goals. What can Drew do to achieve his retirement dreams?

Improving Your Business Hygiene

In our first illustration, there were a couple of easy first steps that Tim could take in order to become more attractive to the opposite sex: brush his teeth and take a shower. Without these two actions, Tim would never get any dates, no matter how successful and loving he was.

This concept also applies to your business. There are major turnoffs to buyers that are not hard to correct but can make a big difference in attracting suitors. In addition, there are a couple of situations that are such major turnoffs that the business owner must resolve them before placing the business on the market.

Let's stick with the dating analogy. In today's world, Internet dating is very popular. It is unfortunate, but true, that someone on the other side of a computer will size you up in minutes based on your online profile. Your online profile is your first impression to a sea of potential suitors.

First impressions are important. You don't get a date with a bad first impression. For most potential buyers of your business, their first impression of your business is your web site. Remember the last time you searched the Web for a service (house or carpet cleaning, accountant, home improvement, and so on)? I am sure that some web sites were inviting and you wanted to know more about the service, while others were uninspiring and you immediately clicked to the next site.

It is important that you have a web site that will not turn off a buyer. It would be better not to have one than to have a web site that looks like you spent 30 minutes developing it from a 1995 template. Your web site will be the first impression that potential buyers will have about your business. Make sure that it is inviting enough for them to want to pursue you in person.

The second hygiene issue is the look and feel of your business facility. When you are looking to buy a house, "curb appeal" is important. When I am in the market for a house, I know within seconds whether I have interest or not due to "curb appeal." Like a house that is for sale, your business facility projects an image to potential buyers. When potential buyers arrive in person for the first time, does your facility attract them or repel them? How do they feel about your business when they leave? Was it chaotic and sloppy or professional and exciting? Just like a first date, buyers will leave their initial meeting with a specific impression, and it may not accurately reflect the true nature of your business. Before putting your business on the market and having buyers visit your facility, make sure that your facility is clean and organized. Add a fresh coat of paint and new carpet, eliminate the clutter in the office, and get rid of any potential offensive images on your walls.

Consideration   Will having a better web site and a nice-looking and well-organized facility increase the dollars that you get in a sale? Maybe not, but it will increase the number of suitors you will have.

After potential buyers get past their first impression of your web site and facility, there are other very significant hygiene issues that will have an impact on their desire to pursue your business further. How well your business performs back office tasks (billing, collections, and paying vendors) is very important to buyers. After they buy your business, they want to focus on selling and making a product. They don't want to waste time and energy on the back office issues. The more confidence that buyers have in the efficiency of your back office, the more attractive your business will be to them.

There are a few situations that will make it very difficult for you to sell your business or force you to sell at a fire-sale price. These issues must be resolved before placing your business on the market, and they include a major lawsuit, negative publicity that has been broadcast in the media, the loss of a major customer, and defective product and warranty issues. Once you've taken care of those issues, allow some time to elapse from the event before putting your business on the market.

Even if you are not selling your business, addressing these basic business hygiene issues can improve your business's cash flow. An inviting web site will drive business. Cleaning up the facility may allow for productivity gains. A functional back office will allow you to bill and collect receivables quicker. These are important areas to address. However, the real increase in your business value comes from increasing your future cash flows and reducing business risks.

Increasing Your Sustainable Cash Flows

Investors buy future cash flow. They look at your business like it is a cash machine. Any actions taken that increase the future cash flow of your business will increase its value. Investors love to buy cash flow that is repeatable and can grow in the future. There is a three-pronged approach to increasing your sustainable cash flow:

- Increase your revenues.
- Improve your gross margin percentage.
- Lower your operating expenses.

We will discuss strategies on how to increase your revenues and grow your business later in this chapter (see the section on "Developing a Growth Plan"). For now, I will focus on the last two items.

Improve Your Gross Margin Percentage

The most important item on your financial statements to a potential buyer is your gross margin amount and percentage. Gross margin (or gross profit) is the difference between the product selling price and the cost to produce or acquire a product. It measures what is available to you to cover your operating costs and provides you with profits after factoring the costs to make a product. Operating costs include expenses like office wages, rent, advertising, and professional fees. The gross margin percentage is simply the gross margin divided by revenues.

The following is the gross margin level amount and percentage for Sensational Snacks:

Revenues	$ 6,000,000	100.0%
Cost of Goods Sold	4,200,000	70.0%
Gross Margin	$ 1,800,000	30.0%

The cost of goods sold for Sensational Snacks includes the raw materials (potatoes, wheat, cooking oil, and salt) as well as factory wages, facility expenses, equipment costs, and delivery expenses. Determining the cost of goods sold is more difficult for a manufacturer than for a retailer. For a retailer, it is simply the cost to buy the product that is sold to the customer. It is important that you compare your gross margin percentage to others in your industry to see how you stack up. (The best source to find this information is a trade association for your industry.) Also, your gross margin percentage trend is critical when valuing a business. A rising gross margin percentage makes your business more valuable.

There are two ways that you can increase your gross margin percentage. You can either raise the selling price of your products or lower the cost associated with making your products (material and labor):

- *Raise the selling price*: In today's competitive market, it is difficult to raise prices. Price increases across the board do not work. Instead, you should analyze each product or service offered and selectively raise prices on items where demand is strong and competition is weak. Also, you can raise your price if you can increase your customers' perception regarding the value of the product or service that you offer. If you can demonstrate to your customers that your products and services are superior, then you can charge a premium. Starbucks has been very successful with this strategy. This is how they get customers to pay double for what others charge for a cup of coffee.

- *Lower the cost of goods sold*: You want to make sure that you are producing or acquiring your products in the most efficient way possible. By lowering your material waste and labor costs, your gross margin percentage will increase. I have seen amazing results from clients who have adopted a Six Sigma or lean approach to making a product or delivering a service. From this, they gained significant efficiencies and have seen their gross margin levels increase. In addition to becoming more efficient, you should carefully study how you purchase raw materials. Lowering the prices you pay for raw material costs will increase your gross margin percentage. You can do this by comparison pricing between vendors, seeking volume discounts, and, in some industries, by using a few hedging strategies.

You will see increases in your gross margin percentage if you selectively increase prices and become more efficient in delivering your product or service to your customers. A small change in your gross margin percentage will have a large impact on value.

Let's look at how a change in the gross margin impacts Sensational Snacks' value. Drew slightly raises the prices on two of his most popular snack lines. He was also able to reduce product waste and increase his production line efficiency after hiring a lean Six Sigma consultant. Sensational Snacks' gross margin percentage has increased from 30% to 32.5%. After these changes, notice the impact on Sensational Snacks' net income:

Revenues	$	6,000,000	100.0%
Cost of Goods Sold		4,050,000	67.5%
Gross Margin		1,950,000	32.5%
Operating Expenses		1,300,000	21.7%
Net Income Before Taxes		650,000	10.8%
Income Taxes		227,500	3.8%
Net Income	$	422,500	7.0%

Drew's gross margin percentage increased from 30% to 32.5% and the gross margin level increased from $1.8 million to $1.95 million. How does this impact his value? Here is the new enterprise value after this change:

Sustainable Net Cash Flow	$	422,500
Required Rate of Return		25.0%
Enterprise Value	$	1,690,000

With only an increase of 2.5% in the gross margin percentage, the value of Sensational Snacks increased from $1.3 million to $1.69 million. It was well worth Drew's efforts to focus on improving his gross margin percentage.

Lower Your Operating Expenses

Operating expenses are the costs to operate a business that are not related to producing a product or delivering a service. These costs include office rent, administrative wages, advertising, telephone, utilities, entertainment, and professional fees. Sometimes these costs are called general and administrative expenses or overhead.

It is easier to identify potential cost savings in operating expenses than it is in the cost of goods sold. Looking for the cheapest phone service or coming up with strategies to lower travel costs is much easier than gaining efficiencies at producing a product or delivering a service. Most businesses run a fairly tight ship when it comes to operating expenses. During the recent downturn in the economy, most business owners had to lower their operating expenses in order to survive.

Business owners can become too focused on lowering their operating expenses and hurt their business value down the road. Some operating expenses are necessary to keep you in business (rent, telephone, and office wages), and you should make sure there is no waste in these items. However, there are expenditures that you make that can improve your business value. It makes sense to spend $20,000 on a lean Six Sigma consultant if it will result in a $400,000 increase in the value of your business. Certain expenditures will provide you with a great return on investment including hiring consultants to improve efficiency, preparing annual valuations, and developing a strategic plan. Spend your operating expenses wisely. Cut the expenses that are not needed to keep you in business and that do not increase your business value.

One of the biggest mistakes business owners make is having the business pay for personal expenses. Vacations, vehicle expenses, and relatives on the payroll who do not contribute may provide you with some tax savings, but they also lower your business value. If you are planning on selling during the next few years, I suggest that you forgo those personal perks that you have your business pay. That "business trip" that really was a $30,000 vacation may cost you $120,000 in value. Remember that the price you receive in a sale is a multiple of your cash flow. You may be able to explain to the buyer that the $30,000 business trip was not necessary and should be added back to earnings. Some buyers may agree with you, while others will not. Why risk it? Eliminate personal expenses that are not typical in your business.

Important   Do not treat your business like your personal "piggy bank." Avoid having the business pay for your nonbusiness personal expenses. Not only will you sleep better knowing that you are in compliance with the tax law, you will receive more cash proceeds when you sell your business.

Going back to our example, let's see how lowering operating expenses will impact the value of Drew's company. He has decided that the company will no longer have the business pay for all of his vehicles and vacations. In addition, he determined that he was overstaffed by one administrative person and proceeded to eliminate that position. With those two steps, he was able to reduce his operating expenses by $100,000. The following is his revised income statement after improving his gross margin percentage and reducing his operating expenses:

Revenues	$ 6,000,000	100.0%
Cost of Goods Sold	4,050,000	67.5%
Gross Margin	1,950,000	32.5%
Operating Expenses	1,200,000	20.0%
Net Income Before Taxes	750,000	12.5%
Income Taxes	263,000	4.4%
Net Income	$ 487,000	8.1%

The combination of increased gross margin and reduction of operating expenses has increased his net income from $325,000 to $487,000. Here is the new enterprise value after these two changes:

Sustainable Net Cash Flow	$	487,000
Required Rate of Return		25.0%
Enterprise Value	$	1,948,000

Drew's value just keeps growing. The increase in value due to the increase in the gross margin percentage and lowering operating expenses is $648,000. Certainly it was worth Drew's time and effort to devise strategies to increase his gross margin percentage and lower his operating expenses.

Reducing Your Business Risks

As stated earlier, there is an inverse relationship between your business value and the required rate of return needed to entice an investor to buy your business. The higher rate of return required, the lower the business value. I explained in the previous chapter that the required rate of return is a function of business risk. Business owners must understand this concept. Reducing business risk is the area where I believe business owners have the most control in affecting value. Earlier, I discussed strategies to increase your cash flow; however, the marketplace may prevent a price increase or it may not be possible to reduce your costs to make a product. Business owners can reduce business risk with the proper focus and strategies.

Why does risk lower value? It is because risk causes uncertainty about the future cash flows of the business. Once you truly understand how specific risk factors impact your value, you will be motivated to establish a plan of action to reduce your business risks. The steps involved in reducing your business risks are as follows:

- Identify all of your business risks.
- Quantify how each risk factor impacts your value.
- Prioritize which risk factor you want to focus on.
- Develop strategies and action plans to reduce the risk associated with each risk factor.

Some risk areas will take years to address while others can be minimized by simply purchasing insurance or making the right hire. Based on my experience, the following six areas are the most prevalent risk factors that impact business value:

- *Employee issues*: This is the most common issue that I add a risk premium for. Most privately held businesses have thin management teams and rely on a few employees to drive business performance. The loss of a key employee can significantly impact the company's future cash flow. It is imperative that you build a strong management team and lessen the reliance on any one employee. In order to keep key employees, provide them with market compensation and a long-term incentive plan that rewards their performance. All key employees should have employment and noncompetition agreements. In addition, you may want to buy "key person" life insurance on certain employees. Your most important strategy in this area is to make yourself obsolete. This will significantly lower your risk and provide you with more freedom. If you don't take this step, you will not be able to leave the business when you sell it. The buyer will have to retain you until you can be replaced. This not only reduces your value but will put you in the uncomfortable position of taking orders from someone else. It rarely works out for the seller.

- *Customer concentration*: In Chapter 3, I told the story about a company that had $90 million of its $100 million in revenues with one customer. The company's value vanished when it lost this customer. Besides employee issues, customer concentration is the most common risk factor. The level of the risk premium associated with customer concentration issues depends on the following factors:

  - Is there a long-term contract with the large customer? If so, the risk premium might be reduced.

  - Why does the customer buy from your business? If it is simply based on price and the customer has many alternatives, then the risk premium is higher. If the customer buys because the product or service is unique and hard to duplicate, then the risk premium is lower.

- How healthy is this customer? Is the company near bankruptcy or financially sound?

- Does the customer buy based on a relationship with an employee at the business? If so, will the customer stay if that employee leaves the business?

The buyer or the valuator not only needs to understand the amount of revenues that come from the large customer but also quantify the true risk factor. At times, I have not placed a high risk premium for customer concentration issues. This happens when the risk level is mitigated by a long-term contract or by the fact that the client's product is unique and needed by the customer.

- *Low barriers to entry*: Companies with low barriers to entry are more risky than those with a high barrier to entry. How easy is it for a competitor to enter your market? You may be making a ton of money, but if it is easy for a competitor to grab your market share, it is unlikely that the cash flow will be sustained. A good example of this is web page development companies. In the late 1990s and early 2000s, there were a few large companies that focused on developing web pages for businesses. They did quite well for a few years, but then most of the larger companies in this industry went bankrupt. Why? They created very large organizations with significant overhead, but the cash flow was not sustainable. The barriers to entry in the industry were very low. Soon, advertising companies and individuals were competing and the prices to develop web pages dropped significantly. I am not discounting the skill and importance of this service—I'm simply making a point. To get into this business, no license or college education is needed, and there is very little out-of-pocket costs. If you are skilled in this area, all you need to get into business is a computer, a business card, and the ability to market yourself. Compare this to a business that has a significant amount of intellectual property that is protected and requires millions of dollars of investment to get established. There are very few individuals or businesses that have the resources to compete with Apple or MGM casinos.

- *Product sustainability*: Today, products and services become obsolete much faster because of technology advances. If you don't believe this, simply look at the current market value of Research in Motion (the manufacturer of the Blackberry). It is currently worth 10% of its value five years ago. Why? The iPhone and Android phone technology has displaced the Blackberry. In order to determine the risk level for product sustainability, it is important to perform an analysis of where the company's products are in the life cycle. Are they mature products in a highly competitive market, or is it new technology that is legally protected and will not face major competition in the coming years? To lessen your risk and make your business more valuable, make sure that you protect your products and processes and any other intellectual property legally.

- *Inconsistent financial performance*: Investors love cash flow that is repeatable when making an investment. If there are two companies that have averaged $500,000 a year for the past five years in earnings, which one of the following do you prefer? The one that has earned $500,000 each year for the past five years, or the one that had earned $2 million two of the past five years and lost $500,000 the other three years. Most investors would choose the former. The more volatility that you have in your historical earnings, the higher the risk premium.

- *Litigation exposure*: Litigation is a fact of life for business owners. This risk area, if managed properly, will not impact the value of a business. It is important that you have the right insurance coverage to protect you from product liability, malpractice, employee issues, and other business risks. A lawsuit against a business that does not have the proper coverage will impact value. The impact level depends on the size of the lawsuit and the probability of a judgment against the business. The same is true for violations against governmental agencies' rules and regulations. A large EPA fine or assessment from the IRS will negatively impact your value. You can lower your risk by being diligent in complying with the governmental agencies that govern your business.

There are many other areas where a risk premium would need to be applied, including the following:

- Too much reliance on one supplier

- Labor availability and strife

- Government regulations that will impact future business

- Negative working capital and other balance weaknesses

- Aggressive competitors

We have seen Drew increase his value by increasing his gross margin percentage and lowering his operating expenses. Drew has decided to further increase his value by reducing the risk associated with his business. The first thing he does is to establish a plan to make himself obsolete in the business. He hires a human resource consultant to assess the leadership abilities of his management team. It is determined that his daughter has the ability and desire to take over Drew's CEO role. She enrolls in an executive MBA program and hires a business coach to expedite her progress. In addition, the sales manager and the plant manager sign employment and noncompetition agreements. With these changes, buyers will feel more comfortable that the business could survive without Drew. In addition, they will not worry about his key employees leaving and competing. With these changes, the required rate of return needed to entice a buyer is reduced from 25% to 20%. The following shows the impact on value with this risk reduction:

Sustainable Net Cash Flow	$ 487,000	$	487,000
Required Rate of Return	25.0%		20.0%
Enterprise Value	$ 1,948,000	$	2,435,000

A change from a 25% required rate of return to 20% has made a big impact on value. The value has increased by $487,000! Drew is motivated to reduce his other major risk. He decides to no longer be so dependent on one customer. He hires an aggressive sales person who develops new markets for his products. In addition, he stops selling his low margin products to his 30% customer. This combination reduces the largest customer's sales to 15% of total revenues, and the top three customers now comprise only 30% of the revenues. By doing this, Sensational Snacks' profits are no longer at the mercy of the three largest customers' whims and demands and Drew's earnings are more repeatable. By lowering his customer concentration and making his earnings more repeatable, Drew has reduced the required rate of return to 15%.

What is the value of Sensational Snacks assuming a 15% required rate of return?

Sustainable Net Cash Flow	$	487,000
Required Rate of Return		15.0%
Enterprise Value	$	3,247,000

Drew's hard work to reduce his business risks has really paid off. The value of Sensational Snacks has increased from $1.95 million to $3.25, million with the reduction of the required rate of return from 25% to 15%. The required rate of return reduction is due to Drew proactively reducing the company's reliance on himself and the one large customer.

▨ **Important**   Business owners should identify the risk factors associated with their business and have specific strategies and action plans in their strategic plan to reduce these business risks.

Developing a Growth Plan

The buyer's perception of your future growth rate will impact the value of your business. The higher the expected growth rate, the higher the value of your business. You can increase the value of your business by developing a strategy to have sustainable profitable growth.

The compound annual growth rate (CAGR) measures the annual growth of a business over a certain period of time. What is most important is the buyer's perception of future growth. The best way to improve that perception is to have a few years of CAGR higher than others in your industry. There is no better combination than a high historical growth CAGR and the expectation of continued growth. In a hot industry, growth is easier than a mature market. Most industries are mature, and growth has to come from taking business away from competitors or developing new products.

Of course, growth can come from buying another company. If you have a strong desire to grow quickly, this may be a good strategy for you. Is it better to buy growth or to have organic growth? Growth through acquisition can be an effective strategy if you don't overpay and have a well thought-out implementation strategy. In most surveys about business transactions, less than 50% of acquirers are happy with the results of an acquisition. Why is that? They either overpaid or did not properly integrate the acquired business into their existing business.

When clients engage me to assist them in buying a business, I tell them to spend as much time in developing integration plans as they do in the pursuit of the deal. It is sort of like getting married. Many spend more time planning their wedding than figuring out how to live together in harmony for the rest of their lives.

Which should you pursue: organic growth or an acquisition? With some analysis, you will be able to answer this question. If your business has an opportunity to buy a company for $1 million, would you be better off buying it or spending $1 million trying to duplicate what you are buying? Prepare an analysis to determine the answer. Many are surprised by the end result and forgo their acquisitions plans, putting all their efforts into organic growth.

With the recent worldwide economic downturn, there is a hunt for growth for most companies. Growth is hard to find. What can you do to increase your chances of obtaining sustainable growth? There are three basic growth strategies to consider:

- *Market penetration*: This involves selling more of your products and services into your existing market. You develop a plan to obtain more customers through advertising, efforts of your sales force and channel partners, or price reductions. This is the easiest strategy to develop but usually does not create sustainable profitable growth. You are essentially just stealing customers from your competitors. The other problem with this strategy is that sales growth may come at the expense of your gross margin. You create value by increasing your gross margin percentage. Getting into price wars to gain market share lowers your gross margin percentage.

- *Product development*: For many, the best way to increase revenues is to develop new products or services that you can sell to your existing customers. Apple is the master at this strategy. Many of my friends have four or five Apple products and will buy the next thing that the company sells whether they need it or not. This can be much more profitable than stealing customers from your competitors. However, it comes with more risk and will cost you time and money to develop new products and services that may not be accepted in the marketplace. It is imperative that you spend a significant amount of time and analysis in determining if the marketplace really wants your new product or service before using this strategy.

- *Market development*: This strategy entails expanding your geographic reach, including international sales. With the advent of the Internet, this strategy is now available to many more businesses. You need to perform a good cost-benefit analysis before committing to this strategy. If it will cost you $300,000 to open up a new office in a different location, how much product do you have to sell in order to break even? Will you become distracted by the new location and lose focus? Can you maintain the same quality control in a different location? These questions need to be answered before proceeding with this strategy.

Buyers are attracted to you when you have a growth strategy you can articulate and there is traction in moving that strategy forward. They also are impressed when you are able to show them that you have a firm grasp about your marketplace. You should know what your market share is and, more importantly, your potential market share.

The final piece of increasing Sensational Snacks' value is to implement a growth strategy. Drew develops a strategy to add a gourmet potato chip line and sells it to existing customers. It has been accepted by some of his customers and will increase his revenues by $300,000. The following is the new income statement after all of the changes discussed have been implemented. His net income has increased from $325,000 to $551,000.

Revenues	$ 6,300,000	100.0%
Cost of Goods Sold	4,253,000	67.5%
Gross Margin	2,047,000	32.5%
Operating Expenses	1,200,000	19.0%
Net Income Before Taxes	847,000	13.4%
Income Taxes	296,000	4.7%
Net Income	$ 551,000	100.0%

The long-term expected growth rate has increased by 1%, which lowers the rate of return required by an investor to 14%. The value of Sensational Snacks with these changes is as follows:

Sustainable Net Cash Flow	$	551,000
Required Rate of Return		14.0%
Enterprise Value	$	3,936,000

Drew's Newfound Freedom

The combination of increasing cash flows, lowering business risk, and increasing sustainable growth is very powerful. Sensational Snacks is now worth $3.94 million which is over three times the original value.

Can Drew retire? Assuming a tax and transaction cost of 30% of the enterprise value, Drew's net proceeds from the sale of his business would be $2.76 million. His liquid assets have increased from $700,000 to $3.46 million. This along with his $500,000 of real estate brings his net worth close to $4 million. Drew is since now he is able to retire at the lifestyle that he wants. But now, interestingly, he is unsure if he wants to retire. He enjoys going to work more than ever and may put off retirement for a couple of years. Instead, he will fund his retirement with the additional profits, making it possible to gift the business to his kids. By treating his business "like an investment" and increasing its value, he no longer feels stuck and has many different options to choose from.

Before concluding this chapter, I would like to make one last point in making your business more attractive to potential suitors. If you are thinking about selling your business in the next five years, it is important to make your business look as professional as possible.

Professionalizing Your Business

What does it mean to professionalize your business? It is simply giving the impression to a buyer that your business has the look and feel of a well-oiled machine. It provides buyers with additional confidence that they are making the right decision to buy your business. There are three main areas that will make your business more professional and more attractive to a buyer:

- *Upgrade your accounting and legal service*: Which provides a suitor more comfort—financial records in a shoebox or an audit from a large reputable CPA firm? Business owners thinking about selling their business should have an outside accounting firm provide them with either reviewed or audited financial statements. An audit provides the highest level of assurance and a review is the next step down. It is also important to engage a seasoned business lawyer to review and update your buy-sell, employment customer, and other important agreements. Many business owners have the same CPA and lawyer that they started with. Make sure that the professionals on your team are the best ones to get you through the selling process. It may not be your golfing buddy or your spouse's cousin who will be effective at making this happen.

- *Employee manuals and job descriptions*: A buyer wants to be confident that the business will continue to be profitable after a transaction. It is not unusual for there to be some turnover of employees once a transaction occurs.

What creates the future cash flow? Employees! Buyers feel better about buying a business that has employee roles and responsibilities well documented. This makes it easier to replace someone and keep the cash machine moving forward. The more roles and procedures that are documented, the more assurance buyers will have when they buy your business.

- *Identify and document your intangible assets*: Intangible assets are critical to the success of all businesses. You want to make sure that buyers understand what they are buying when they purchase your business. They will know that they are buying inventory, fixed assets, receivables, and some intangibles (e.g., customers and patents). However, many intangibles assets are much harder to identify. You need to communicate to a buyer all of your intangible assets that your business owns, such as the following:

    - Market research you've conducted

    - Processes and formulas for making products

    - Your approach to customer service

    - The relationships you have in the community and industry

    - Experienced employees

    - Proprietary products and processes

    - Proprietary software that you have developed

It is worth your effort to document your intangible assets and legally protect the ones that you can (patents, trademarks, and copyrights).

Summary

There are ways you can make your business more valuable and attractive to potential suitors. Hopefully, the end result of what happened to Sensational Snacks has provided you with some motivation to develop plans to increase your business value. There are three key areas that you can focus on to increase your business value:

- Increase your sustainable cash flow.

- Reduce your business risks.

- Develop a growth plan.

As part of your strategic plan, develop strategies and action plans in each of these three key areas. Small changes can make a big difference in your business value. Also, improve your business hygiene and make your company look more professional. You will attract more potential buyers, which will drive up the price of your business.

In the next chapter, I will walk you through the process of selling of your business from the time you decide to place your business on the market to the closing of the deal.

Selling Your Business

Who Will Get Your Baby?

"Bruce, this is the last client that I will act as an intermediary for in selling a business." I wish I would have said that one project earlier.

In 1999, my partner and I decided to expand our consulting practice to include the service of selling businesses for a success fee. The majority of our fees were based on whether we successfully located a buyer for our clients' businesses.

It is a service that I no longer provide. The experience that I gained providing this service was invaluable and has enabled me to provide better advice to business owners about valuation and succession issues. Since I gained experience in dealing with the realities of the marketplace, I am now able to advise my clients from "real-world" experience instead of a merely academic point of view.

We closed many deals, and it was a high-risk, high-reward service offering. When a business sold and the seller received the price that he wanted, everyone was happy and we got paid a lucrative fee. Other times, we spent a significant amount of time and resources on a deal that was never consummated and we did not receive a success fee. Most of the time, deals did not close because we did not find the right buyer willing to pay the price the seller wanted. Other times, we found the right buyer at the right price, but the sellers backed away at the last minute because they were not emotionally ready to sell.

After seven years of providing this service, I decided to focus exclusively on valuation and succession-planning consulting services. I enjoy this work more, even though it is less lucrative. When we sold a business, we obtained a fee that was significantly higher than a consulting fee based on our hourly rates. Of course, if a deal did not close, the opposite happened. The feast-or-famine fee arrangement was frustrating in that it provided unpredictable income. However, that wasn't the most troubling aspect.

I knew providing this service was risky. When people buy a business for millions and it doesn't work out the way they hoped, they like to point fingers. Usually, they don't point their fingers at their own decisions.

When I reluctantly agreed to take on the engagement I decided would be my last, I did not realize it was going to be part of my life for seven years and that I would be a defendant in a lawsuit for the first time in my life.

The lawsuit was settled while writing this book, so it is very fresh in my mind. We were sued three years and eleven months after the deal closed. The statute of limitations for professional services in Ohio is four years. Because of a confidentiality agreement, I cannot provide you with specific details of the engagement, but I will give you with an overview and describe the crux of the case.

The company that we represented was in the housing industry and was very successful. The deal closed in the winter of 2007, only a couple of weeks before the collapse of the housing market. The sellers that we represented started a similar type of business in the western part of the United States and decided they wanted sell their business and focus on their new companies.

The engagement started about one year before closing. We received a letter of intent (LOI) from the eventual buyer within weeks of being engaged by the sellers. Once the LOI was accepted, the buyer proceeded to perform due diligence over the next 60 days. The due diligence process did not go very well. The buyer came back and said he found many things that caused him concern and would agree to buy our client's company at a significantly reduced price. My client was not too thrilled with the reduction in price, and we tabled the deal for a few months. A few months later, we reopened negotiations and the parties eventually agreed on a price. The attorneys then went to work on an asset purchase agreement and after a few hiccups, the deal eventually closed.

Within 90 days of the deal closing, the sellers were informed by the buyer's attorney that they had violated the clause in the asset purchase agreement about providing accurate financial statements. The sellers provided financial data for a four-year period as an exhibit in the asset purchase agreement. The buyer claimed that one number was materially wrong on the latest financial statement provided. These statements were prepared by the sellers' internal accountant and were not reviewed or audited by an outside accountant. We made it clear to the buyer that we did not provide any assurance about their financial records and that the buyer needed to conduct his own due diligence. The buyer hired a financial expert to examine the company's financial records.

The sellers sued the buyer to recover the monies held in escrow and demanded a good portion of the purchase price back. After a couple of years of battle, the sellers declared bankruptcy. The housing industry collapsed, and the epicenter of the collapse was the location where the sellers started their new business and invested the funds from the sale. Their personal fortunes were gone. During the lawsuit against our client, our records were subpoenaed and I was deposed. After it was clear that nothing could be recovered from the sellers, the buyer proceeded to sue us to recover his claims of damages. The discovery period lasted almost two years, including a dozen depositions in five different states. It was a very time consuming and emotionally draining process. Fortunately, I had a great support system with my family, friends and fellow partners at Rea & Associates—for which I am forever grateful.

My intention is not to scare you off from selling your business. I was involved with many deals that went very well and where both the buyer and seller achieved their goals, including those where the seller received tens of millions of dollars. It is very fulfilling to be part of the process that assists business owners in selling their business to the right buyer, enabling them to retire rich.

The perspectives that you will receive in this chapter come from both the "thrill of victory" related to successful deals and the "agony of defeat" regarding the ones that did not go so well.

The Best Time to Sell Your Business

The majority of business owners will eventually sell their business. Few will give it away to family members or simply shut down the business when they exit. With this in mind, when is the best time to sell your business? If the following is all lined up perfectly, you will be able to sell your business at the optimal price:

- Your sustainable cash flow has peaked.
- Your business risks are at the lowest level.
- Your forecasted growth is at its highest level.
- Bankers are lending money freely at great interest rates.
- The overall economy is doing well.
- Income taxes on business transactions are favorable.
- There are buyers available that have significant cash levels.

- There is aggressive buying of companies in your industry.

- You are able to find fulfillment and sense of purpose outside the business.

If all these factors are aligned perfectly for you today and you want out, don't hesitate. Place your business on the market and reap your rewards!

But it's not as easy as it seems. I have seen everything aligned perfectly for an industry only once in my career. This was in the late 1990s for the technology industry. The economy was humming, the infancy of the Internet was driving growth and profits to record levels, and there were irrational buyers in the marketplace. Companies were buying others based on multiples of revenues and not profits. The sellers were becoming millionaires though their companies had never achieved a profit. Then someone woke up and questioned the valuations of all the technology companies. The stock market crashed, and the economy slowed down. If the company mentioned in Chapter 2, started the selling process only one month earlier he would have received $5 million from a large technology client. Post-crash, he never received an offer over $1 million. Timing is an important consideration when selling your business.

You have no control over several of these factors (e.g., macroeconomic and banking trends). However, it is important that you understand that these factors will impact the price you get for your business. They may also impact your timing in selling it. Ask yourself this question: "Is the overall selling climate optimal now or will it likely improve in the future?"

At all times, you should be diligent in growing your business value and not be so worried about the general economic factors outside of your control. If you do this, then you can try to time the market to optimize your price. Of course, if you are not ready to leave (emotionally or financially), then continue to work on growing your business value until you are ready.

■ **Important**   Concentrate on growing the value of your business while understanding how outside factors impact the best time to sell your business. This will allow you to maximize the price you will receive for your business.

Before walking you through the process of selling a business, I will discuss the current state of affairs for selling a business and the typical terms in a business deal.

Current State of the M&A Marketplace

Many advisors and publications use the term "M&A" (an abbreviation for mergers and acquisitions) when discussing the industry and marketplace of selling companies. Therefore, I will use this term when discussing the selling process. The number of M&A transactions and the prices paid for companies is down significantly since the year 2007. Experts call this "M&A sluggishness." This is true worldwide, and I have seen this sluggishness in my consulting practice. It is due to the worldwide recession that started in 2008. During the past four years, most of the M&A activity in my practice has come from individuals that sold for personal reasons or wanted to take advantage of the low capital gains that expired December 31, 2012.

The recession has reduced companies' profits, cash flows, and growth prospects. The banking crisis has also restricted a buyer's ability to borrow money, which raises the cost of capital (required return of investment) on business deals. The combination of lower cash flows and higher cost of capital has reduced values. In addition, sellers are receiving less cash at closing due to the banks' reluctance to fully fund deals. Buyers are requiring more monies to be held in escrow and seller financing to close a deal. Why the M&A sluggishness over the past few years? It is the combination of lower valuations due to the recession and the lower investment returns on alternative investments. Over the past few years, the business owner has been better served by retaining the business and restoring its value rather than selling it and then earning less than 1% on the net proceeds placed in a savings account.

Periods of M&A sluggishness is why you need to always be ready to sell your business and treat it like an investment. You want to be ready to sell when the M&A marketplace is robust. If your goal is to sell your business at the highest possible value, you have to consider what is going on in the M&A marketplace in general.

I am optimistic that the M&A market will recover. There are so many business owners who want to sell their businesses right now but can't because they will not be able to retire on the after-tax proceeds. The recession may have delayed M&A activity, but it did not stop Father Time. As business owners get older, they will need to execute their exit strategy soon. There are willing and able buyers on the sidelines waiting to make a deal. Per many published reports, there is a record level of cash that publicly traded companies are holding on to. The combination of a supply of sellers and record cash levels of potential buyers will trigger a nice recovery in the M&A marketplace, assuming an economic recovery and bank stability.

Timing the selling of your business is like surfing. When you hit the wave at the right time, it is quite a ride. If there is no wave, you are stuck going nowhere—or paddling on your surfboard.

■ **Important**   If you want to sell your business during the next few years, be ready for the next wave in M&A activity. If you miss it, it might be another few years before you can ride the next wave.

The Terms of the Deal

Selling a business is unlike any transaction that you have ever experienced. The largest transaction that most people have been involved with is real estate. Selling your house can be complex, but it is child's play compared with selling a business. The price and cash you receive from selling your house are easy to comprehend. There is a closing statement that spells it all out. Also, it is clear what is being sold: your house and specific contents that have been identified in the simple three-page real estate contract. The same cannot be said about a business transaction.

When you sell your business, you will come to an agreement on the price for the business with the buyer. The next question to ask is this—how will the price be paid? It is rare when it is similar to a real estate purchase in that 100% of the price is paid at closing. The typical components of the payment for a business include the following:

- The majority of the price is paid in cash at closing.

- A portion of the price is held in escrow.

- The seller may finance a portion of the deal by accepting a note from the buyer.

- The price may increase due to an earn-out clause.

- A consulting, noncompete and employment agreement is often included.

As a seller of your business, you want as much of the deal price as possible to be in cash at closing. The buyer wants the amount of cash paid at closing to be as little as possible. The amount paid at closing is part of the deal negotiations.

It is typical that a portion of the deal price will be placed in escrow to allow for a reduction in the price after closing for either a violation of the purchase agreement or buying an asset in which value is in question (e.g., the true value of accounts receivable). The amount placed in escrow is typically 10% to 20% of the purchase price for a 90- to 180-day period. The funds are held by an independent escrow agent and will be released to the seller once the buyer gives the escrow agent approval to release the funds.

Most buyers like the seller to have some "skin in the game" after they sell the business and to remain financially attached to the deal. This can be accomplished by a seller's note, an earn-out and a covenant not to compete.

- *Seller's note:* Many times, the seller will have to finance part of the purchase price. Buyers may need to bridge the gap between the purchase price and their own resources and the amount the bank will lend on the deal. The note covers the difference. The seller's note is subordinate to bank financing, and you should always try to secure the note to a buyer's reachable asset. I warn my clients to have the mindset that they may not collect the entire value of the note; thus, they should make all their financial plans based on cash received at closing. The note should never exceed 20% of the purchase price.

- *Earn-out:* An earn-out is the portion of the purchase price that is paid after closing based on reaching certain milestones previously agreed upon. This means the ultimate purchase price can increase if the buyer meets the goals spelled out in the earn-out. An earn-out is used when there is a valuation gap that needs to be bridged or when there is a large risk factor that concerns the buyer. For example, in Chapter 3, we discussed the client that had 90% of its revenues from one customer. A possible earn-out in that scenario is that a large portion of the purchase price is contingent on that main customer remaining for a specified time period.

    Often, the buyer and seller cannot come to an agreement on the ultimate purchase price, but they would like to move forward. An earn-out gives sellers the ability to achieve the price they want and provides buyers some assurance that they have not overpaid. Performance-based earn-outs may be based on revenues, gross profits, EBITDA, or net income. I prefer that earn-outs be based on revenues or gross profits since the EBITDA and net income levels are subject to manipulation by the buyer. Early in my career, I was an expert in a litigation case where the buyer and seller had an earn-out arrangement based on the EBITDA levels. The seller never collected on that earn-out because the buyer proceeded to take out a $1 million salary and there were no profits left in the company to pay the earn-out.

- *Covenant not to compete:* In the majority of business deals, the seller is required to sign a covenant, as part of the transaction, not to compete. Most buyers would never buy a business if the seller could collect cash at closing and open up a competing business across the street. There usually is a separate value assigned to the covenant promising not to compete and is considered part of the total deal package. In addition, the seller may receive either a consulting agreement or an employment agreement as part of the deal. The buyer will want the seller's expertise to assist in the transition process. Sometimes, this is included in the purchase price, and other times it is a separate contract signed at closing. Buyers like to shift some of the purchase price to a consulting agreement for tax purposes.

What Are You Selling?

The answer to this question seems to be simple: your business! But it's not that simple. Will you be selling your company's stock or business assets? Will all of the business assets transfer to the buyer or just the goodwill, inventory, and equipment? Which party is responsible for the company's liabilities? These questions will be answered during the negotiation process and documented in the purchase agreement.

As a seller, you will want to sell your company's stock (stock deal) because you will then relieve yourself from any obligations that may arise from the past. Plus, there is a huge tax advantage. However, the buyer typically does not want to buy your stock but would rather buy business assets and assume as few of your liabilities as possible (asset deal). During my career, about 95% of sales transactions have been asset deals.

In a stock deal, the shares of stock of the business are transferred from the seller to the buyer, as well as all of the assets, liabilities, and operations. Also, any skeletons that may arise from the past (i.e., tax issues, product warranty, employee suits) will be the buyer's responsibility. There are major tax disadvantages for the buyer in a stock deal. The business assets depreciate in the same manner as they did before the transaction, but at a rate that is lower than it would be under an asset deal. Also, the buyer is not able to write off any of the purchase price as a tax deduction. In a stock transaction, the buyer assumes more risks and has a significant tax disadvantage. It is rare when you find a buyer who is willing to do that.

In an asset deal, the seller retains ownership of the stock of the company. The buyer must either create a new entity or use another existing entity for the transaction. Only assets and liabilities that are specifically identified in the purchase agreement are transferred to the buyer. Other than some specified liabilities, such as accounts payables and lease obligations, all other liabilities of the company remain with the seller. This means if a lawsuit arises from an event prior to the closing of the deal, sellers will have to defend themselves out of their own funds. After selling the business under an asset deal, the seller liquidates the business entity and then receives the proceeds personally. Buyers record the assets and liabilities at the fair market value assigned to them as part of the transaction. This allows buyers to have greater annual depreciation of the fixed assets purchased, which lowers their income taxes. Unlike a stock transaction, the buyer will be able to write off any value assigned to goodwill as well as any other intangible assets over a 15-year period.

The seller's tax consequence under an asset deal is usually much higher than under a stock deal. Sometimes the difference is significant. Because of the importance of this topic, we will discuss this further with an example at the end of this chapter.

The Steps in Selling Your Business

The process of selling your business is more complex, emotionally draining, and time consuming than selling a house. It is important that you are mentally ready for the uncertainty and stress that goes along with it. Have a timeline in your mind for when you would like to sell your business, but be flexible. Find someone you can trust who has either been through the process or has assisted others that you can talk with confidentially and openly while you are selling your business.

The following is the typical order of events that occur once you decide to place your business on the market:

- Select your transaction team.

- Locate the buyer.

- Sign a letter of intent.

- Enter the due diligence process.

- Negotiate the asset purchase agreement.

- Close the deal.

Before placing your business on the market, you want to be able to articulate your reasons for selling and you should also consider telling your key employees.

Many owners are reluctant to tell their key employees that they are selling the business. They fear these employees will run out the door searching for a new job if they hear that the business is for sale. One client told me that his biggest concern about placing his business on the market was that his employees would find out. He and his wife were 80 years old and frail. But actually, the employees were scared he would not sell the business and that it would be liquidated after his death.

I believe that it's important that you inform your key employees of your intentions. They will likely sense that something is going on. Rumor and innuendo can make them leave faster than hearing the truth. Articulate why you are selling, assure them that you will tell the buyer how important they are to the business, and properly incentivize them to stay. The incentive that is popular in this situation is a large retention bonus that is paid to the employee(s) after the deal is closed.

Can you state your reasons for selling? Prospective buyers will want to know your reasons. Planned retirement or wanting to cash out and accept a new challenge in your life are some of the best reasons for selling. This provides some comfort to the buyer that there are no hidden business reasons for selling the business. Whatever the reason, make sure you can confidently explain it since buyers naturally wonder—if the business is so great, why are you selling?

▓ **Important**　Keep the end in mind during the selling process. You are exiting for a reason so don't let your emotions derail you from your financial and personal goals. Find someone you can trust during the process to be a sounding board and provide you with an objective perspective.

Select Your Transaction Team

It is important that you select the right advisors to be on your team. Once the deal is closed, there is no turning back. For most, this will be the largest and most complex transaction that they will be a part of in their lifetime. You will need trusted, experienced advisors to assist you and be able to provide you with their full attention. Figure 6-1 shows which advisors are needed and how they interact with each other:

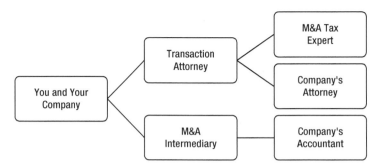

Figure 6-1. These experts are needed for an M&A transaction to allow the best chance for success

Before placing your business on the market, obtain an independent valuation that provides you with a value both for an investment value standard (synergistic buyer) and a fair market value standard (financial buyer). This valuation will provide you with some assurance of the validity of the offers you receive. You want someone independent providing you with the valuation and not the intermediary whose compensation is tied to the sale of the business.

■ **Note** A synergistic buyer is someone in your industry—maybe a competitor—who will buy your business for its product lines, sales channels, to eliminate competition and so forth. Synergistic buyers may fold your business into their own, putting people out of work and closing facilities. Financial buyers, on the other hand, are wanting to employ their capital and may be looking for a new challenge, an out-of-work corporate executive, etc. They are more likely to keep the business intact.

The person that you hire to find the buyer and quarterback the process has many different names in the business community, including investment bankers, business brokers, and intermediaries. Investment bankers typically handle very large transactions (in excess of $100 million), and business brokers deal with smaller transactions ($1 million or less). M&A intermediaries handle transactions in the middle, though both brokers and investment bankers sometimes dip into this territory as well. Throughout this chapter, I am going to use the term "intermediary" to define the advisor who will quarterback the process.

The intermediary has many different roles in the selling process. His main job is to find the right buyer for you, quarterback the entire process, and be the buffer zone between you and the buyer. It is a critical role. You want this person to create competition among buyers to drive up the price in a confidential way. Intermediaries need excellent communication and problem-solving skills and the patience of a marriage counselor. After obtaining a letter of intent

(LOI), the intermediary will work closely with you and your accountant in the due diligence process. When you move to the purchase agreement, they will work in conjunction with the transaction attorney to make sure the agreement aligns with your wishes.

The transaction attorney also has a very important role: *to let you sleep at night after the deal is closed.* Studies have shown that less than 50% of buyers are satisfied with an M&A transaction. There are various reasons why so many are dissatisfied—they may believe they paid too much for the business or that they did not fully understand how the business operated. They may also feel that they were misled by the seller regarding the health of the business.

Even if you disclosed everything possible and the buyer had complete access to all materials, there is still a chance that the buyer will try to negotiate a lower purchase price or try to recover some of the proceeds paid to you. The transaction attorney's role is to document your wishes in the purchase agreement and to limit your exposure to future litigation or recovery of funds once the deal has closed. They will work closely with your corporate attorney to ensure all legal issues have been disclosed. They also will work with the M&A tax expert to ensure the purchase agreement properly documents the tax treatment of the transaction. If the IRS ever questions the tax treatment of the deal, they will use the signed purchase agreement as the starting point in their investigation.

Finally, you will want to retain an expert in the M&A tax field. You need someone who really understands M&A tax issues and has years of experience. As you will see later in this chapter, a mistake in how taxes are treated in an M&A transaction will cost you dearly.

Remind your advisors that they work for you. Deals can get derailed if attorneys and other professionals have their egos hurt during the M&A process. When it gets nasty, they could easily lose sight of their client's goal.

▨ **Critical**   Make sure that the professionals on your team understand their role and that their job is to accomplish **your ultimate goal—a successful sale**. You are the one in control of this process.

Locate the Buyer

You will need to decide whether you want to pursue a synergistic buyer, a financial buyer, or both. The key difference is that synergistic buyers will pay more for your business because they can achieve higher cash flows than you can through cost reductions or increased margins. Synergistic buyers are typically larger companies in your industry. Financial buyers will probably continue the business in its present form. A financial buyer can be someone inside your business (including an ESOP), a family member, or an outside investor.

You will have to decide whether obtaining top dollar for your business is most important or whether the continuation of your legacy is a must. You rarely accomplish both of these goals with one buyer. The process of determining your exit strategy and your personal goals is discussed in Part III. Once you choose which type of buyer is the best for you, you can develop a strategy to find the right buyer. If the buyer is outside of your company, you should work closely with the intermediary on developing this strategy. If you know that the buyer is an internal buyer, there is no need to hire an intermediary.

The intermediary will develop a marketing plan and send out a "teaser" about your business to develop interest. The teaser should not disclose your identity and should be discrete. Make sure that you review what is being sent out about your company to potential buyers.

Hopefully, the intermediary will have a robust response to this initial marketing campaign. The intermediary should screen potential buyers before providing them with any additional information. The screening process includes making sure the buyer is financially sound. Nothing is more frustrating than to spend months on a deal and find out that the buyer is not able to close the transaction due to lack of funds. You may want to screen out specific companies or individuals to whom you don't feel comfortable giving access to your financial information. This could be your biggest competitor or someone who bought your friend's company and did not keep his promises.

Once you are confident that the potential buyer has adequate financing and you feel comfortable with releasing financial information about your company, the prospective buyer should sign a confidentiality agreement. It is important that your corporate attorney reviews the confidentiality agreement to make sure it protects you. After the buyer signs the confidentiality agreement, the intermediary will send the buyer a confidential information memorandum (CIM). This document not only discloses your identity but includes a summary about your operations, historical financial results, and your prospects for the future.

The purpose of the CIM is to obtain an offer from a prospective buyer. Hopefully, you will have several offers to choose from and you will receive an LOI that meets your satisfaction.

▓ **Suggestion**   "Date" the buyer before making any commitments. Spend a lot of time with the buyer to make sure this is the right person to take over your baby.

Sign a Letter of Intent (LOI)

Once a buyer is found, it is time for the engagement period. The prospective groom gives his future bride the promise of a great life and his commitment with a ring. A buyer does the same thing with the term sheet or the LOI. Term sheets and LOIs are both preliminary, nonbinding documents that record an agreement between the parties on the major terms of a deal. The difference between the two is simply a matter of style. A term sheet lists the deal terms in bullet-point format, and an LOI is written in letter form. I will use the term "LOI" in this chapter. These key components are a part of this agreement:

- Specifics of what is being purchased, including whether the transaction is an asset or stock deal

- Price and final pay-out at closing

- Agreement about any seller financing or earn-out

- Details of the due diligence process

- Removal of the seller from the market

- Proposal for a closing date

After you sign the LOI, you lose your negotiating power. The price and terms you agreed to in the LOI will not get any better and can become less favorable. During the due diligence process, if buyers find items they do not like, they may try to renegotiate the deal. I have never seen a case where the buyer says, "The business is better than we expected so we are going to offer you more money!"

For a specified period of time, you will have to honor a "no shop" agreement and take your business off the market. However, you don't want the trail to get too cold if there are other interested parties. You need to limit the due diligence process and have the "no shop" agreement become void immediately if the buyer intends to materially change any deal terms. Give buyers a specific time period (less than 60 days) to perform their financial due diligence. I advise sellers to have a meeting with the buyer within 30 days of starting the due diligence process to determine if the buyer has any intention of changing the terms.

■ **Land mine**   Don't sign an LOI until your attorney has reviewed it and you are completely satisfied with all deal terms. The deal will not get any better, and you can lose out on other interested parties if you sign an LOI with a buyer who will not honor the terms.

Enter the Due Diligence Process

This is the most dreaded part of the deal process for the seller and intermediary. They have spent a significant amount of time and energy finding the right buyer and negotiating the LOI, and now someone is going to examine the business with a fine-toothed comb. It is the halfway point, and this is where most deals crumble. The seller will be inundated with questions and requests, all without knowing how the process is going from the buyer's point of view. I have included a sample due diligence request (see Appendix C) in order to provide you with a general idea of what may be requested from you.

It is very important to disclose potential issues and less favorable items to the buyer prior to signing the LOI. It is much easier to negotiate the impact of any bad news on the deal price before signing the LOI rather than after signing it.

Most buyers will ask for a period of 60 to 90 days to complete their due diligence. Negotiate this down to no more than 60 days with a due diligence update midway through the process. Having audited financial statements available will make this process go much smoother and quicker. From the buyer's perspective, the quality of information available about your business is critical. If the buyer is not confident that the company's financial statements reflect reality, the deal will die or be subject to a price revision.

Most buyers will hire experienced CPAs and attorneys to go through the financial and legal records. CPAs will look at the quality of historical earnings and make sure that they are sustainable into the future. They will also examine critical areas such as receivable and inventory values, revenue recognition practices, and tax compliance. Typically, they will issue a written report to the buyer. The attorneys will search for potential legal, employee, and environmental issues and examine critical contracts and intellectual property protection.

Make sure that you involve your corporate attorney during this process. You don't have to provide everything the buyer requests. You may not want to turn over your customer list or your secret formulas during this process. Seek the advice of your attorney if the buyer asks for anything that makes you uncomfortable.

If the buyer informs you that items were found in the due diligence process that will impact the terms of the deal, ask for their findings in writing. Take these findings to your advisors to determine their validity and what impact they will have on value.

Due Diligence Tip   Have a cooperative tone throughout the process and make it easy for the buyer to obtain the requested item. It raises suspicion if you are belligerent and do not respond properly to a valid request.

Negotiate the Asset Purchase Agreement

The Asset Purchase Agreement (APA) is the definitive agreement that finalizes all terms and conditions related to the sale of your company's assets. It is different from a Stock Purchase Agreement, where the stock is sold including all assets and liabilities. Since a wide majority of deals are asset purchases, we will focus only on the APA. Generally, an APA contains the following items:

- The identification of the specific assets being purchased

- The purchase price

- The amount of cash to be paid at closing

- The details of any seller notes or earn-out

- What assets are excluded from the sale

- What liabilities will be assumed by the purchaser

- The date of closing

- Representations, warranties, and indemnifications

- The allocation of purchase price for tax purposes

- Exhibits that include financial statements

We have discussed most of these items. The exception is the representations, warranties, and indemnifications. It is important that you have an understanding of the purpose of these items in the APA. This is the area where the transaction attorneys earn their fee.

Representations and warranties are statements of fact and assurances made by both the buyer and the seller. Buyers want comprehensive representations and warranties to protect themselves against any problems or unforeseen issues. Sellers want to give as few representations and warranties as they can and limit the financial impact if there is a breach. Indemnification provides one party with a contractual remedy for recovering post-closing monetary damages arising from a breach of a representation, warranty, or any other contract issue.

In the deal that I opened the chapter with, the buyer asserted that there was a breach in the seller's representation about the accuracy of the financial statements. The remedy they sought (indemnification) was the release of the escrow funds to their account and an additional payment by the seller to reduce the price paid. When my client refused these conditions, the buyer sued the seller.

Representations, warranties, and indemnification terms are the focus of a substantial amount of time and energy in negotiations. The only way to avoid this is to agree with all of the seller's wishes in this area and have a significant portion of your proceeds from the sale held in escrow. However, this approach is not something I would recommend.

As a seller, your goal is to provide reasonable representations and warranties and limit your indemnification exposure. You can place caps on the damage amount, as well as time limits when damages can be claimed. Different areas of exposure may require different time limits. A financial statement representation may expire after one year, but an environmental representation may last much longer.

■ **Land mine**   Don't minimize the importance of the representations and warranty promises that you make in the APA and understanding the indemnification clause. Don't sign the APA until you are confident that you will not end up in court post-closing.

Close the Deal

This is what you have been waiting for. Sign the APA and get your money! However, most deals do not close upon the signing of the APA, and there can be a small time lag to make sure that the transition from old owner to new owner is smooth. The deal is not closed until you see the funds wired into your account or a check at the closing table. At closing, you will have some deductions from your sale proceeds. Intermediaries receive their fee at closing and other professionals that assisted in the transaction may also insist on being paid at closing. There are no taxes withheld at the closing, and you will need to send what you owe to the IRS based on the recommendations of your tax advisor.

Funds that are held in escrow will be sent to an escrow agent and are released based on the terms in the APA. If buyers make a claim on the escrow funds, they will ask the seller to tell the escrow agent to release the disputed funds to them. At times, there is litigation over the escrow funds. It is important that your APA is very clear about how escrow is released and how disputes are resolved.

The Tax Impact of a Sales Transaction

The saying "don't let the tail wag the dog" applies to the area of taxes on M&A transactions. Taxes are a very important consideration when selling your business but don't let the tax issue drive your decision-making process. Too many business owners fret over taxes rather than growing the value of their business. To retire rich, grow your business. Then when you are ready to sell, hire an M&A tax expert to minimize the impact of taxes on the transaction.

The seller and the buyer have competing interest when it comes to taxes on a deal. Typically, what is good for the seller is not beneficial to the buyer. This is why your tax expert should be brought in early in the process and not at the end of the deal.

In this section, I do not intend to make you a tax expert on M&A transactions. Frankly, this area is too complex for me, and I rely on tax experts in my firm for all M&A transactions. The point I want to make is how important it is to have a tax expert assist you through a transaction. To emphasize this, it's helpful to look at best- and worst-case illustrations.

Each different legal form of business (C-Corporation, S-Corporation, LLC, and Partnership) has different rules in regards to M&A transactions. Regardless of the legal form of business, the gains on a transaction are either classified as ordinary income or a capital gain. The tax rate difference between ordinary income and capital gains is significant, and there are specific rules from the IRS for what classifies as ordinary income vs. a capital gain.

In 2013, the tax rate increased for high-earning individuals in the United States. Here is a summary of the highest individual tax rates for 2013:

Capital Gains and Dividends	20.0%
Medicare Surcharge on Investment Income	3.8%
Earned income	39.6%

In order to understand the tax consequences on a sales transaction, I will continue with the example of Fantastic Footballs, Inc. At the end of the last chapter, Charlie's business was worth close to $4 million and we will assume that he receives an offer of $4 million. The two examples that follow demonstrate the difference between a stock sale and an asset sale.

With these calculations, I will assume the highest 2013 tax rates (ignoring the impact of state and local income taxes) and that Fantasy Footballs is a C-Corporation. For a stock deal, sellers recognize a gain based on the difference between the sales price and their current basis in the stock. Basis is the owner's original investment. If you did not buy your business, the basis of your stock is usually minimal. For this example, Charlie's stock basis is zero. The gain is taxed at the capital gains rate along with the new Medicare surcharge tax on investment income. The federal income tax calculation for the stock transaction is shown here:

Selling Price of Stock	$ 4,000,000
Individual Stock Basis	-
Taxable Gain on Transaction	4,000,000
Capital Gains and Surcharge Tax	23.8%
Federal Taxes on Transaction	$ 952,000

Charlie will have to pay $952,000 in federal income taxes. That's a lot of money. However, it gets worse under an asset deal.

Now let's look at the tax treatment of an asset deal. There is one additional assumption that we need to add. Each asset that a company owns has a tax basis, which is usually the asset's original cost less any depreciation. We will assume that the tax basis of the assets being sold is $2 million. The company receives a check for $4 million and will have a $2 million taxable gain on the transaction. The company has to pay taxes on the difference between the selling price of the assets and the amount on which the assets are recorded on the books for tax purposes (tax basis). After paying the corporate tax on the transaction, business owners then have to pay taxes on the amount that is sent to them personally after the transaction is closed.

In this example, the company owes $680,000 in taxes from reporting a gain on the sale of the assets. The only asset that Fantastic Footballs has now is $3.32 million in cash. Charlie liquidates the company and receives the $3.32 million as a dividend, and he has to pay taxes on that amount at the individual level. Based on the 2013 tax law, Charlie's federal tax rate on this distribution will be 23.8% (dividend rate and Medicare surcharge on investment income). He will owe $790,000 individually on this distribution. The combined corporation and individual tax from the transaction is $1.47 million.

Selling Price of Net Assets	$ 4,000,000
Corporate Basis on Assets Sold	2,000,000
Corporate Gain on Transaction	2,000,000
Corporate Income Tax	34.0%
Federal Taxes on Transaction	680,000
Income Tax on Individual	790,000
Federal Taxes on Transaction	$ 1,470,000

The difference in the income tax bite between an asset deal and the stock deal is huge! It is $518,000. Now this is the worst-case scenario. If Charlie hired a good tax expert, there are legitimate strategies to lower the tax bite of the asset deal.

Tip   The basic rule of thumb in M&A transaction is to have as much of the taxable gain classified as a capital gain rather than ordinary income. If the buyer will not allow a stock deal, have your tax advisor show you areas where you can achieve capital gains rates on an asset deal.

Other business entity forms (besides a C-Corporation) do not have to worry about the double taxation issue (except some S-Corporations that were once C-Corporations), but there is still a battle over what is classified as a capital gain and ordinary income.

Both the buyer and the seller will have to include Form 8594 to report the sale to the IRS. On this form, the total selling price of the business is allocated to the various asset classes transferred in the sale. The values entered on the seller's and buyer's copy of Form 8594 must be identical.

My Top Ten Tips in Selling a Business

To end this chapter, here are my top ten tips when it comes to selling your business:

1. Don't wait too long. Exit your business from a position of strength, not weakness. It is important to sell before you become bored with the business, or worse yet, an illness or retirement forces a sale.

2. Have a reasonable expectation on the price that you desire for your business. Since an inflated figure either turns off or slows down potential buyers, rely on a valuation expert to help you arrive at what your company is truly worth. Do not set a price for your business. Instead, have buyers provide you with a price that they are willing to pay. They may surprise you with a price higher than your expectations or true value.

3. Don't let taxes drive your actions but don't neglect their impact.

4. Engage a team of experienced M&A professionals. This is the best way to obtain the highest selling price, minimize your tax burden, and allow you to sleep at night after the deal is closed.

5. Prepare for the sale years in advance. This includes having audited or reviewed statements at your disposal from years back and updating important legal documents.

6. Achieve a higher price through buyer competition. Hire the right intermediary who can create a competitive situation with buyers. The more buyers bidding for your business, the higher price you will obtain.

7. Be flexible. Don't be the kind of seller who wants all cash at the closing, who won't accept any contingent payments, or who insists on a stock transaction.

8. Disclose potential negative factors early. Make sure that there are no unpleasant surprises for the buyer during the due diligence process. This will save you time and money and avoid killing a deal or renegotiating a price at a lower value.

9. Don't let time drag down the deal. To keep up momentum, work with your intermediary to be sure the buyer adheres to a strict time schedule.

10. The line from an old song is true for the M&A process: "You got to know when to hold 'em, know when to fold 'em." If the market or your gut is telling you that this is not the right time to sell after starting the process, pull the plug, reassess, and start the process again when the time is right.

Summary

The most popular exit strategy is the sale of a business. The majority of business owners will eventually sell their business, and it's most likely to be the largest and most difficult transaction in their lifetime. It's not the time for saving fees by using inexperienced professionals or going through this process alone. The amount received on the sale of your business will impact your financial future.

M&A activity ebbs and flows. It is important that you are ready to enter the market at the right time. The best time to sell is when your business and M&A activity are strong. It is important to have your business in a saleable position in order take advantage of peaks in the market.

Make sure that you have the right professionals on your team. You will need an experienced intermediary, tax professional, and a transaction attorney. Each one has a critical role to play but remember that you are the one who is in charge of the process. Do not ignore the impact on income taxes when you sell your business. You can lose 50% of the purchase price to income taxes with an improperly structured deal.

If you are unsure if selling your business is the right exit strategy for you, please read on. We will discuss how you can exit your business on your terms in Part III.

Getting Out Alive: Planning Your Exit

The Hardest Step: Succession Planning

What Will Your Legacy Be?

The advisor across the table could tell that his client, an 80-year-old widow, was having a hard time with the estate plan he presented her. He thought the plan met her personal wishes, saved her a ton of estate taxes, and would benefit a charity she loved. After all, it was not easy developing a plan for a widow with $20 million in liquid assets. It was the perfect estate plan for her, and he was puzzled by her worried look.

Are You Kidding Me?

He asked her, "Why are you hesitant to move forward with the plan presented?" She said, "I am not sure if I can afford to give a $5 million gift to a charity I love." The advisor was puzzled. She still would have $15 million left over after the gift, and she lived a conservative lifestyle. It would benefit both the charity and save her over $2 million in estate taxes. The advisor decided to probe deeper and ask a few questions. Finally, after asking several more questions and patiently listening to her answers, the advisor got to the bottom of the issue. The widow told him, "I heard that nursing homes are very expensive, and I am worried that I will run out of money if I have to go into one." The advisor, thinking quickly, said, "Okay, let's take $1 million of your remaining $15 million and buy a nursing home. Then you can stay for free."

Did she actually buy a nursing home? No. The advisor was simply making a point, and she ultimately proceeded with the plan.

Doesn't it seem ridiculous that a person with $20 million in liquid assets was worried about nursing home costs? It does, but this situation shows how difficult succession and estate planning can be. In highly emotional situations, it is easy to lose perspective. If someone studied any of our lives, including my own, there would be areas where our thought processes and actions would seem ridiculous.

Why Is Succession Planning So Hard?

Typical business owners put a lot of blood, sweat, and tears into their business. They sacrificed much to get where they are and have a huge emotional attachment to their business. They are good at making products, growing the business, and dealing with customers. But the whole concept of exiting the business is foreign to them. Succession planning forces them into uncharted waters. Why should they spend time and money on something that is so far away from implementation?

It is not hard for all business owners. For those who want to die at their desks, succession planning is easy. It is also easier for those who plan to sell their business to the highest bidder and then move to a tropical island and forgot about the business forever. They just have to worry about building value in the business and exiting at the right time.

For those who want the business to continue once they leave, it is not such an easy process. There are complex legal and financial issues to figure out (estate plans, retirement needs, legal documents to ensure plans are carried out, etc.) and equally complex soft issues (choosing the next leaders, dealing with sibling rivalry, giving up control, etc.). They must figure out a way to leave and not kill the goose that lays the golden eggs (the business).

Business owners who want the business to continue must be willing to face difficult business, personal, and family issues in order to start the succession-planning process. There are conflicting goals. What is good for you personally may not be what is best for the business and other family members. In addition, there are other stakeholder needs that must be addressed with succession planning (employees, other shareholders, customers, and the IRS).

In order to be successful, you have to make sure that your business can continue without you, maintain family harmony, and sort out your own personal desires. Figure 7-1 illustrates these issues that must be addressed:

Succession Plan

Figure 7-1. The health of the business, family issues, and the desires of the business owner are three critical succession issues

Business Health

Whether business owners want to gift their business to the next generation or sell it, they must leave the business in the best shape possible. A healthy business has the right leadership team, a strong financial position, and good business strategy.

The most important issue the business owner must deal with prior to exiting the business is determining the next leader. Transitioning leadership is not the same as transitioning ownership. They do not have to be done at the same time.

The most meaningful task that business owners can focus on prior to leaving is to make themselves obsolete. Real value is created and succession is much easier when the business is no longer dependent on the owner for anything.

■ **Tip**   As the business owner, never forget that you have an important job: to make yourself obsolete. Making yourself obsolete adds to the value of your business because it means you have key people in place, giving the new owner peace of mind.

The business also should be on a firm financial foundation prior to the owner leaving. The new leadership team should have enough breathing room that a mistake in strategy or an unexpected event does not drive them out of business. This can be hard to do since leaving significant financial resources in the company may mean less money business owners can extract from the business to fund their retirement.

Finally, make sure that the next leadership team has a well-defined business strategy to pursue. One of the final tasks you should perform prior to leaving the business is to hire an outside consultant and go through an in-depth strategic planning process with the new leadership team. They will need your wisdom to point them in the right direction and periodic follow-up visits to discuss strategy and the issues facing the business.

Family Issues

The complexity of family issues varies, depending on the number of family members involved in the business and the nature of those relationships.

I recently advised an Amish family business that had ten kids in the business. It was one of my most unique and enjoyable engagements. I have never consulted with a business that had that many second-generation children in the business. This is usually a difficult situation that makes it hard to come to a consensus since there are so many people with different needs. However, there was a single-mindedness among the family members that made the process easy. They all wanted to be paid fairly for their specific roles, have the most qualified people in charge, and then share the profits equally. Most situations with that many family members in a business are not that easy.

Bad choices in selecting family members to be leaders will kill the business. I know of a multigenerational business that had tens of millions in revenues that is no longer in business. The company had a rich history, but it had to be sold at a distressed price. The CFO of the company was a family member with no formal accounting training. Everyone thought the company was doing fine based on the financial statements. Unfortunately, the financial statements were wrong, and for the past couple of years the company had been losing money. Once it was discovered, it was too late and the company could not recover. I wonder if anyone had ever questioned the patriarch's decision on having an untrained family member as his CFO?

Many times it is clear whom you should choose to be the next leaders in the business once you are gone. When it is not, it is important that you be as objective as possible because a poor choice will kill the goose that lays the golden eggs.

▓ **Critical Issue**   The selection of the future leaders in your business should be based on objective evidence that they will be successful and not based on nepotism.

Personal Issues

In addition to the tricky family issues, the business owner must face difficult personal issues during the succession-planning process. For many owners, much of their life's work and personal identity is tied up in the business. Very difficult questions, including thinking about your own mortality, will have to be addressed and answered during this process, including the following:

- What am I going to do with myself once I leave the business?

- How will my decisions impact my relationship with my spouse and kids?

- Will I have enough money to live the lifestyle I desire?

- Will I be happy playing golf every day? How will I spend my newfound free time?

- Will the business survive without me?

These are hard questions to answer, and not all business owners who successfully exit from their business in terms of dollars are content with their new life. I know of a very successful business owner who sold his business for millions of dollars. Within a year of the sale, he was working in a department store selling suits because he did not know what to do with himself.

Important But Not Urgent

In Chapter 1, we discussed Stephen Covey's time management matrix and how successful people make sure that they spend a significant amount of time in Quadrant II (important but not urgent issues). When you own a family business, it's easy to get caught up in the day-to-day activities. It's much easier to deal with customers and employees than to think about your own mortality and how your decision about your exit will impact scores of employees. No one is pressing you to decide and communicate your succession plan. Most like to avoid having those important, strategic discussions with your family about the future of your business.

But there is a certain point in time when you must decide that it is time to start down the path of succession planning. And once you make that step make sure the succession planning process becomes both important and urgent to you. The urgency is not that it has to be done today, but working on your succession plan is now a repetitive appointment on your calendar. Procrastination, you will realize, is not the answer and may be detrimental to your family and employees.

Why Waiting Will Not Make It Better

When I am facing a difficult issue, I like to procrastinate. You never know ... it may get better with time. No need to see the doctor, the pain should go away. No need to talk to my boss about the angry client, she will cool down. Seeing an attorney about my will can wait. What is the chance that both my wife and I will die at the same time?

When I procrastinate, I have this feeling that there is something hanging over my head. The problem may be swept under the rug, but I do not feel free. One of my favorite Greek mythology stories is the sword of Damocles. (It is not that I am a big Greek mythology fan; I learned about this story from an episode of *The Three Stooges*.) The story provides some insight on how there is a lack of peace when there is something hanging over your head. It is told by the Roman politician and philosopher Cicero and the key players are the ancient ruler of Syracuse, Dionysius II, and his courtier Damocles.

Dionysius was very powerful and wealthy, and Damocles was jealous of him. Dionysius decided to switch places with Damocles so that Damocles could experience what it was like to have power and wealth.

Dionysius' power and wealth were transferred to Damocles. However, as part of the deal, Dionysius arranged to have a huge sword hang above the throne, held at the pommel by only a single hair of a horse's tail. With this sword hanging over his head, Damocles could not enjoy his newfound power and wealth and decided that he no longer wanted to be so fortunate. From the outside, he saw the good things associated with having these privileges. But he did not count the cost of the responsibilities.

The point of the story is that there is no peace for those who wonder when the sword will fall on their head—no matter how much success and money they may have.

The business owner that avoids dealing with the succession process is like Damocles. No matter how much success they have, the question remains. How are they going to get out of their business alive and well? This will always be hanging over their head like the sword over Damocles. Here are a few situations that may cause the thin string to break:

- A key employee leaves.

- An illness incapacitates you.

- Chaos in your family unexpectedly happens that changes your succession plans.

- An unforeseen world event occurs like 9/11.

- A competitor introduces a new product.

Having a plan does not guarantee success, but knowing the direction you are heading does make the string holding the sword stronger.

Stories of Procrastination

It is rare when procrastination is a good thing, but sometimes you can get lucky. One of my clients is an oil producer, and he keeps delaying making gifts to his children. He was one of the few lucky ones. It turns out that his wells are located in an area where there are significant newfound oil reserves. I have prepared four valuations for him in order to gift his shares to his kids. Four times he has failed to make the gifts. Recently, he was offered over five times the value of his company because of the newfound oil reserves that are located deep below the location of his wells. Sometimes procrastination works! But most of the time it doesn't. There are many more stories without such a happy ending.

During the past 20 years, I have seen numerous business owners lose millions of dollars due to procrastination. One example was a 95-year-old very successful business owner. At our initial meeting, I asked him about his estate plan. He replied, "My estate plan is to live to 150." I thought he was joking, but I really didn't know. Two years later, I prepared a valuation for his estate, and the estate had to pay millions of dollars of estate taxes. His procrastination cost his family millions.

Also, I have seen family rifts grow larger and intolerable situations arise that could have been prevented by proactive planning. During one engagement, a son displayed to me his bitterness toward his dad. He was complaining about his dad's lack of trust in him. How could he say that his dad did not trust him if he was gifting him the control of the company? This action showed that the dad trusted him. The problem was that the son was 63, and his dad was 87. After the son served over 40 years in the company, and as president for the last 20, the dad finally felt that the son was worthy to have stock. The procrastination of the dad caused a rift in their relationship.

What Will Your Legacy Be?

This past month, I was consulting with a client who owned a business worth over $20 million. He said that one of his advisors asked him, "Why waste your time and money developing an exit and succession plan? You will be dead and won't care. You can let others take care of it after you die." This is a good plan if you don't mind the chaos it creates for your family members, the destruction of your wealth as it goes into federal coffers, and the tarnishing of your legacy.

Legacy is one of those words that is hard to define. It has different meanings to different people. Therefore, it is important to define how I will use it in this book. When I use the word "legacy," I am referring to whatever you leave behind to be remembered by—whether it is money, memories, or your impact on the lives of others.

■ **Legacy**   Whatever you leave behind to be remembered by. It can be money, memories, or your impact on the lives of others.

What type of legacy do you want to leave behind? Is this something you have ever thought about? What is the most important thing you want to be remembered by or for? These questions need to be answered before starting the succession-planning process. Once you determine what you want your legacy to be, you are ready to discuss your exit strategy.

The following are client legacy statements that they have expressed through words or through their actions:

- "I want my son or daughter to continue what I have started and have them pass it down to the next generation."

- "I don't care how I am remembered or how my decisions impact others. Just show me how I can get top dollar for my business."

- "My business is being held in stewardship for my Creator, and my decisions will impact others in this and the next life."

- "I want to sell the business for as much as possible to ensure that my family's future is ensured."

- "It is more important to me that my employees have jobs in the future, and I will take less money on a sale to ensure that."

For some, this process is not very hard because they know immediately what they want their legacy to be. For others, this process will take years of soul-searching. At the end of the process, what is vital is to keep this in mind:

■ **Key Succession-Planning Concept**   It is critical that you align your desires and your life purpose to your succession plan.

Succession-Planning Steps

I am not a "canned program" type of advisor. Also, I don't believe if you follow certain steps you will be guaranteed success. People and situations are complex, and the business world is volatile. There are no guarantees that if you follow certain steps or use a certain program that you will exit your business on your terms.

The accounting, insurance, and law professions are starting to recognize the huge opportunity in succession-planning consulting. Often, I am approached about a new system or software program that I can incorporate into my practice that will make the consultation process easier and allow me to sell more succession-planning services. It is tempting to buy these programs because it would make my job easier. Checking boxes and letting a software program produce a report is much easier than fully understanding the business owner's situation and diving into hard emotional issues. Having a canned presentation is easier than tailoring a plan from scratch. It is also more profitable. However, it doesn't feel right to me and in my opinion does not provide the client with the best outcome.

With that being said, I am going to provide you with some guidelines and steps that should be performed to have the best chance of success. In Figure 7-2, six important steps are listed in the succession-planning process. How you approach each step is up to you, but each needs to be accomplished to have a plan that works. The steps in this figure are in the order of my preference (starting from the bottom and moving upward) since I believe each one builds on each other.

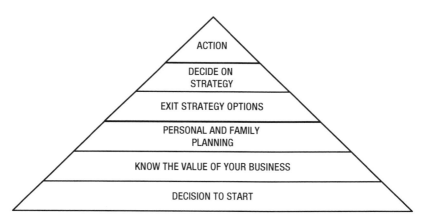

Figure 7-2. Following these critical steps in succession planning (starting from the bottom and moving upward) will give you the best chance of successfully exiting your business on your terms

Decision to Start

This is so elementary—why even put this down as a step? It is the easiest step to do but the hardest step to start. This is because most business owners do not know how to start the process or even where to start.

The best place to start is to put it on your schedule and set aside time to work on your plan even if you do not have a clue what you are going to do during the scheduled time. Maybe for the first few months, your goal is simply to learn all you can about the process. Set a deadline of between one to two years to choose your exit strategy and then design your succession plan. Schedule at least one full day each month into your calendar to work on your succession plan and dive into the process. On an annual basis, take a mini retreat to focus on this plan. It is helpful to have someone assist you in this process and hold you accountable in seeing it through.

Establishing your plan won't tie you to one solution for exiting your business. It is understood that the plan will be a "living document" that you will definitely revise as your life circumstances change and as the marketplace changes. But having this road map in place will make it easier to react to these life changes and choose which path in the road will best meet your needs.

As the old saying goes, "Failing to plan is planning to fail." Improve the chances that you will be able to "exit on your terms" by beginning the succession-planning process.

■ **Tip** Make an appointment with yourself and put it on your calendar—Tuesday, May 14, 9:00 a.m.: Start thinking about succession planning.

Know the Value of Your Business

Earlier in this book, the importance of knowing the value of your business and, in general terms, how to value your business were discussed. Therefore, this section will be short as I emphasize one last time the importance of investing in a business valuation.

■ **Important** Don't be blindsided by unrealistic expectations about the value of your business. Invest in a professional business valuation.

The business valuation should be done early in the planning process and must be done before you can fully understand your exit options and choose a strategy.

As you will see in the next chapter, there are different valuation conclusions based on which exit strategy is chosen. It is helpful to have a valuation that shows how the value changes based on the different exit strategies.

Personal and Family Planning

Laying every family member's goals and desires out on the table is vital in the succession-planning process and for the future of the business. But it's not always an easy process. Often, family relationships can bring sensitive issues to planning sessions. However, communication between you and your family members becomes an essential ingredient of a successful business transition.

I find that family business owners often make critical decisions about the company's and their family's future without first talking with other members of the family. The owner may have decided to pass the business down to the oldest son or daughter and start down that path, only to find out later that the child's dream is to become a lion tamer and will not be involved with the business in the future.

A better approach is to develop a family strategic plan. This is much like a business plan but addresses the business owner's and the family's desires for the future. It also allows each person to have opinions about the future of the business and provides a way for all voices to be heard.

It is helpful to use an outside advisor that you trust to facilitate and document the plan. I like to start the process by providing each family member with a questionnaire and then interviewing them individually. This provides the best opportunity to make sure that all sensitive topics and issues are identified. In order for this to occur, it is important to assure everyone that individual responses will be held in confidence. After gathering this initial information, a group meeting is held to openly discuss the future of the business and what each family member's role will be in the business. It is the facilitator's job to make sure that no one person dominates this process and that everyone's personal goals and concerns are heard.

A well-defined family strategic plan that is interwoven into the business stra-tegic plan will build communication and team building among your employees. This can lead to increased productivity with the employees and happier family members.

Developing a family strategic plan begins by answering some very specific questions. Early in the process, it is important to see if there is a consensus of the best exit strategy for the family. If it is determined that it is best to sell the business to an outside party, then the follow-up questions are very different than if the consensus is to transfer to the next generation.

If the goal is to transition the business to your children or to other family members, then you must determine who wants to come into the business and what the rules will be for employed family members. It becomes important to develop policies and criteria for hiring family members into the business and developing a family creed that sets specific criteria (See Appendix D for a sample family creed). You'll also want to address family members who do not wish to be involved in the business. How will they be treated fairly in the estate?

These key questions should be asked when developing a family strategic plan:

- What is the family vision for the future and growth of the company?

- When is the optimal time to exit the business and why?

- Which exit strategy is the most attractive?

- Who should be the future leader of the business?

- How do we remain unified as a family when making difficult business decisions?

- How can the family have a positive impact on the employees and community?

- What influence should family members who work outside the business have on the future of the business? How can they be treated fairly in the estate plan?

Exit Strategy Options

Business owners have only a few options in deciding what to do with their business. The best option for you will depend on your economic needs and what you want your legacy to be. You may desire to gift the business to your kids. But if you have nothing saved for retirement, this option is not practical.

There are only four basic exit strategies for any business owner. Under each option, there are a variety of ways to accomplish the exit strategy and these are summarized in Figure 7-3:

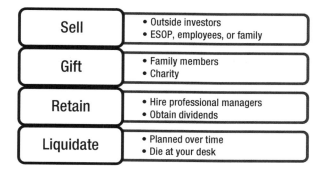

Figure 7-3. Four basic exit strategies are available for the business owner: sell, gift, retain, or liquidate

In the following chapter, I will discuss each of these options in depth, including the advantages and disadvantages of each. I will also walk you through examples that will allow you to compare the economic impact of each strategy.

Decide on Strategy

At some point, you just have to make a decision on how you are going to exit the business on your terms. In Chapter 9, we will pull together all the other chapters and discuss how to decide on a strategy.

Once the decision is made, it needs to be communicated to all the important stakeholders, including your employees, major customers, and professional advisors. Silence brings speculation, and speculation is not just usually wrong but assumes the worst case. If your decision is to sell to the highest bidder in six months, you may not want to shout this from the mountain tops.

The only thing left once the decision is made is setting a plan of action.

Action

You will either pull the trigger on your plan or a trigger will be pulled for you. Eventually you will exit your business, even if your plan is to live to 150. One day, you will no longer be there.

Business owners who fully embrace the steps in this chapter, set a course of action to implement the plan, and seek assistance to ensure the plan is being implemented will see optimal results. This is not guarantee that you will be able to exit on your terms. But if you do not properly plan and set a course of action, outside forces will determine how you exit your business.

▨ **Important**   It is your decision whether you want to exit on your own terms or let circumstances out of your control decide.

One of the first action steps to be performed after your plan is developed is to update your strategic plan and develop a contingency plan. Comprehensive strategic planning without knowing your exit strategy will lead to bad decisions, and you may end up going in the wrong direction. As part of the strategic plan, it is important that a contingency plan be developed. What happens if you must leave the business for an extended period, such as a hospitalization? Or, what happens in the instance of a sudden death? While these things are not enjoyable to consider, you must have action plans in place for the day when you can no longer run your business.

Summary

The hardest step in succession planning is starting. It sounds so simple and easy—like the Nike ad says, "Just Do It." But it is not that simple. This is the hardest step because the business owner must face difficult personal, family, and business issues in addition to the complex tax and legal stuff. There usually is no sense of urgency to start the process, and it is very easy to avoid starting the process.

Your desired legacy is the starting point. In order to achieve this legacy, you need to prioritize the succession-planning process well before your desired time to leave the business. Once you develop your plan, it needs to be communicated to the right people and placed into action—or the sword of Damocles will be hanging over your head.

I would like for you to sleep well knowing that you have done all that you could to create a positive legacy for yourself and for your business.

> *Perhaps the most important vision of all is to develop a sense of self, a sense of your own destiny, a sense of your unique mission and role in life, a sense of purpose and meaning.*
>
> —Stephen R. Covey, from *The 8th Habit: From Effectiveness to Greatness*

Know Your Exit Options

Which Is the Best for You?

"Tim, you will not believe what the prospective buyer said to me," said a client. "The buyer was joking about the sleepless nights my employees will have once they find out that I am selling my business and how they won't know who will survive." This is not the right thing for a buyer to joke about to someone in turmoil about the fate of his employees after he sells his business.

Prior to this phone call, I spent a few months with this client determining his best exit strategy. He had one son who was in the business, but he had quit and was not interested in becoming an owner. Passing the business to the next generation was not a viable option. The owner thought that his only option was to sell the business. But should he sell it to his employees or to one of the three synergistic buyers in the industry? We provided him with one value based on selling to his employees and one based on selling to a synergistic buyer. The difference was significant. In our opinion, he could sell his business for millions more to a synergistic buyer. The synergistic buyer could pay more because the company would move the operations to its own location and eliminate many jobs.

A company in his industry had approached him several times about acquiring his business. After signing a confidentiality agreement, he handed over the requested information and received a very strong offer. I was gratified with the offer since it matched the valuation that we had provided him.

He was torn. Having millions more from the synergistic buyer would set him up for life. But in reality, he would still have more money than he could spend in his lifetime if he sold the business to his employees. Then the fateful phone call happened. The buyer's callousness about his employees caused him to immediately terminate the negotiations. He felt stuck at this point. Even though he loved his employees, they could not write him a check for millions of dollars and it would take years for them to pay him for the business. Were there any other options besides either selling to a heartless outsider or to employees with no cash?

The answer is "yes." In this case, the best exit plan would be a combination of three strategies. The employees would buy some stock, he would make a nominal gift to his two children, and he would retain a controlling interest in the business. The owner will gradually step away from the day-to-day activities and work less hours each year and provide his management team with more responsibilities. He will also provide his management team with equity and cash bonus incentives while either maintaining his large salary or obtaining a significant distribution of the profits from the business each year. A contingency plan would also be put in place in case something happens to him so that his advisors would know what steps to take if he cannot run the business due to illness or death.

This is a plan that he did not envision at the start of the process. But it is a good plan that aligns with what is important to him. All it took for him to determine what was important to him was his competitor joking about his employees losing their jobs. He no longer feels the sword of Damocles hanging over his head (as we discussed in the last chapter).

The End Will Come

At some point, you will have to exit your business. The question is—will you leave on your terms "alive and well" or leave some other way?

A few business owners know their exit strategy on the day they established their business. No analysis is needed to determine their exit strategy. For most, however, it will take years of pondering and analysis to figure it out. And many will never make a choice, choosing by default to let an outside event force their exit.

Do you know your options for exiting your business? The purpose of this chapter is to provide you with information about each exit strategy along with suggestions and tips on how to successfully implement each approach. In the next chapter, we will discuss how you can make the best decision for your situation.

What Are the Exit Strategies?

There are only a few exit strategies that an owner can choose from, though they can be combined in creative ways as shown in the lead story. It is important that you understand all the alternatives and select the one that aligns with your desired legacy and the reality of your situation.

Earlier in the book, we discussed how exit planning consultants often emphasize that only 30% of closely held businesses make it to the second generation. The reality is that most business owners do not want their business to go to the next generation. A 2005 PricewaterhouseCoopers (PwC) Survey[1] verifies this fact. The survey shows that most of the business owners plan to sell their business and only 18% plan to transfer the business to the next generation.

A total of 364 CEOs of privately held, fast-growing US businesses that had revenue between $5 million and $150 million were interviewed. "What was their exit plan?" was one of the questions posed to these CEOs. The results of that question are shown in Figure 8-1:

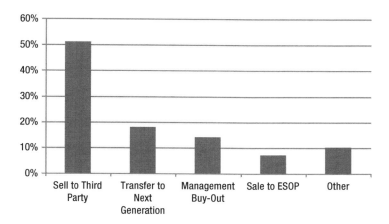

Figure 8-1. The results of the CEO responses on their exit plans are depicted

The survey indicated that just over half (51%) of the CEOs plan to sell their company to an outside third party, while 21% plan to sell to an inside buyer (management or ESOP). Only 18% plan to transfer their business to the next generation.

---

[1] PricewaterhouseCoopers' Trendsetter Barometer, January 31, 2005, www.mbbi.org/info_resources/r_pwcbarometerboomer.pdf.

There are a limited number of reliable surveys available that ask business owners about their exit plans. Even though the PwC survey is one of the better ones, I don't believe it can be extrapolated to all privately held businesses. This survey was only submitted to high-growth companies, and these companies usually have much more opportunities in selling their business. In my experience, the overall results of this survey do hold true: over 50% of the business owners I consult with ultimately want to sell their businesses. In my practice, about one-third of the business owners have the desire to transfer their business to the next generation.

I introduced the available exit options in the last chapter. Within each strategy, there are a number of ways you can accomplish your goals. Business owners are not limited to one exit strategy and can use a combination of these strategies in their succession plan. The client in the introduction of this chapter chose to implement a combination of strategies. He sold and gifted a partial interest and also decided to step away from the business and retain a controlling ownership interest indefinitely.

There are four exit strategies for any business owner. They are listed in the order of popularity in Figure 8-2.

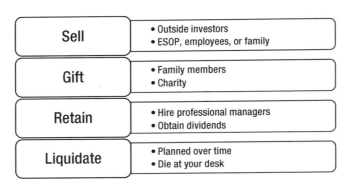

Figure 8-2. Four basic exit strategies are available for the business owner: sell, gift, retain, or liquidate

The remainder of this chapter will be devoted to providing you with further explanation of the different strategies as well as tips on how you can successfully implement each approach. In the next chapter, we will discuss which strategy may be best for your situation and the process you need to go through to make a decision.

Selling Your Business

Because of the complexity and the popularity of this strategy, I devoted an entire chapter about the selling process in Chapter 6. It was important to me that the selling process was explained right after the chapter about how to increase the value of your business. Therefore, my explanation about this strategy will be brief and will focus on how to implement this strategy successfully.

Remember that there are two broad categories of buyers of businesses: synergistic and financial. Synergistic buyers will pay more than financial buyers, but you may not like what they will do with your business once you leave. Usually there are only a few potential synergistic buyers for a business. In fact, it is unlikely that many businesses will be able to attract a synergistic buyer. On the other hand, the universe for financial buyers is unlimited. It could be your employees, family members, or the local executive who recently got laid off from the corporate world.

Whether the buyer is a synergistic or financial buyer, your goal is to make your business as attractive as possible to potential buyers. Having the "investment mindset" toward your business is important in reaching this goal. This mindset is much more important than finding the right time and economic conditions to sell your business.

You cannot always predict swings in the market, and some factors are beyond your control in the optimal timing for selling a business. These factors include current macroeconomic conditions, interest rates, industry trends, and buyer activity. Selling a business isn't just about trying to time the market—it's about timing your business. The absolute best time to sell your company is when your business's estimated future cash flow is peaking and the risk related to the business is at its lowest level.

All too often, when business owners are thinking about retirement, they start winding down their business. They don't pursue that big new client or launch that new product line. Once owners start to mentally "check out," so does their cash flow, which lowers the price at which they'll be able to sell the business. If you're looking to sell, make sure that you remain fully committed to keeping your business healthy while you shop around for prospective buyers. A little extra effort could mean a much bigger payoff in the future, since your buy-out will be based on a multiple of your earnings.

If you know that you want to sell your business during the next three years, remember to focus your energy on the value growth strategies that were discussed in Chapter 5. Focus on developing these strategies:

- Increase the cash flow of your business.
- Decrease the risks associated with your business.
- Create sustainable growth.

There are other things you can do to make your business more attractive and project a better image to potential buyers. Does your business have curb appeal? As buyers visit your web site and your facilities, are they impressed or turned off? As with selling a house, your company's curb appeal can go a long way toward closing a deal.

Implementing the Selling Strategy

Selling your business will be one of the most difficult things that you will ever do. It is complex and time-consuming and will be hard on you emotionally.

Selling a house on your own is difficult, and very few can do this successfully. Selling a business is significantly more difficult than selling a house. Where will you find the right buyer for your business? How will you manage the due diligence process? Are you protected legally during the process? How will you react when the buyer tells you about the warts he found with your business and wants to renegotiate the price?

The selling process is complex, and there are high emotions from both sides of the fence. Smart, highly successful people argue over big dollars. Feathers get ruffled. When I was an intermediary, much of my time was spent keeping a deal moving forward after the parties had a major disagreement. For most business owners, it is very difficult, if not impossible, to sell their business on their own. They don't have the time or skills to look for and locate the right buyer. Even if they could find the right buyer, they would not want to be put in the position of negotiating directly with someone who wants to buy the business for the least amount of money—all the while pointing out all the flaws in the business. It is best for the seller not to be involved in the day-to-day negotiations and to have a representative during the selling process.

Hiring an intermediary or business broker is a good idea when you don't know whom the buyer may be or if there are a number of known potential buyers. The difference between the two is the size of the deal. Business brokers work with smaller businesses (that sell for less than $1 million) and intermediaries work with larger businesses. The services they provide include the following:

- Offering general valuation and market position advice
- Identifying, locating, and screening prospective buyers
- Furnishing buyers with material describing your business and the requested financial and legal documents
- Coordinating the due diligence activities
- Assisting in the deal negotiations and structuring advice
- Overseeing the overall deal management to guide you through the process

If you don't need someone to assist you in locating buyers and you know whom the buyer of your business will be, then an experienced valuation professional or a CPA may be able to assist you through the selling process. It is critical that you hire a tax professional and legal advisor who are experienced in M&A transactions.

One of the most important roles of a broker, intermediary, or valuation professional is to be a buffer between you and the buyer. Buyers want to have their questions answered and be able to express their concerns about the business to someone. This does not make for good conversation with the seller. I have seen many deals go sour because the seller had direct conversations with the buyer.

Make sure that you select an experienced advisor who has significant deal experience. Some advisors specialize in certain industries while others are focused on a certain location. Should you select an industry specialist or someone who knows your geographic area? It depends on who is the best buyer for your business. Do you want to sell to a synergistic buyer for top dollar? If so, an industry specialist is probably best. If your buyer will come from your geographic area, then it's probably wise to use the best advisor in your area.

The typical broker or intermediary will receive a retainer or a commitment fee to initiate the selling process and will also receive a success fee if a transaction consummates. For transactions of less than $1 million, the success fee is based on enterprise value and is typically in the 8% to 12% range. For larger transactions, it is typically a sliding scale based on the size of the transaction. Most M&A advisors will want an exclusive arrangement for 6 to 12 months.

I don't believe that business owners need to hire a broker or intermediary for all transactions. For internal transactions between employees and family members, or if you have identified the right buyer, you may not need to hire an intermediary. The success fee that they earn is mainly for finding the right buyer for your business. But it is still important that you retain the services of experienced professionals to assist you in the selling process. In order for you to obtain and retain the highest proceeds from a sale, you should have a business valuator, tax accountant, and attorney on your team.

As we discussed in Chapter 6, an experienced M&A attorney is an important person to have on your team. The seller will require you to make certain representations and warranties. The purchase agreement will spell out the consequences if you do not fulfill them. Postclosing lawsuits are usually over financial representations or noncompete issues. You have to understand all the legal documents that you will have to sign and make sure that you are protected from a buyer who may have second thoughts about the deal. Most studies indicate that less than half of all merger deals fulfill the expectations of the buyers. Make certain that you will not be held responsible for the seller's inability to achieve their goals for the deal. Of course, if you lied or misrepresented facts, that is a different story and the buyer may be justified in suing you.

■ **Important**   Don't use an attorney who does not have M&A transaction experience. The same attorney who handled your divorce or prepared your will is not the person you want to represent you in a sales transaction. Don't skimp in this area.

Your desired exit strategy may not be to sell your business. You may want your legacy to continue and have your son or daughter take over the reins once you leave. One way to accomplish this is to use the gifting strategy.

Gifting Your Business Interest

If your top priority is passing down your business to the next generation, then you should consider this exit strategy. The transition of your business to the next generation can include gifting your entire interest or a partial interest. It can also include a combination of the gifting and selling exit strategies.

The biggest advantage of the gifting strategy is that your legacy and the business will continue into the future. However, solely using this strategy means that you will not receive a big payout when you leave the business. Therefore, your retirement needs must be taken care of before considering gifting your entire business.

When you make a gift of an interest in your business, you must follow the IRS regulations on gifting. This is true whether you gift a 5% or 100% interest in your business. Also, you will need to look at the impact of the estate tax. Some business owners have been forced to sell their family business due to the impact of this tax.

One of the most famous real-life stories about the importance of understanding the estate taxes involved the Miami Dolphins. Joe Robbie owned the Dolphins and when he died in 1990 his estate was worth about $100 million. His estate tax bill was about 50% of his net worth. The family had to sell the Dolphins at a price lower than its true value in order to pay the estate tax. This was a costly mistake since NFL teams are now selling for over one billion dollars. This situation could have been avoided with proper estate planning that included a gifting strategy.

If you have significant retirement needs, then this option may not be attractive to you. If this is your desired strategy, you need to start planning for your retirement early.

We see the following major dilemma in family businesses when the owner wants to pass the business to the next generation and the children want the business and are ready to take over:

The business owner does not have enough money to retire on, and the children don't have enough money to pay for the "fair market value" of the business.

There are ways business owners can use the gifting strategy and still obtain a return for their hard work and meet their retirement needs. The following are some strategies that you can use to transfer ownership and meet your retirement needs:

- A salary continuation plan
- A deferred compensation plan
- A combination of selling and gifting the business interest

There is a difference between transferring ownership and transferring authority and control in a company. You can decide to take a lesser role in the company, maintain a salary, and still control the company's major decisions. This is done by gifting nonvoting shares or gifting less than 50% of the voting shares to the next generation. You maintain control and can set your salary, benefits, and distribution amounts. Alternatively, you can gift a controlling interest and enter into an employment agreement that spells out your future responsibilities and compensation.

If you want to completely step away from the business but have additional retirement needs, then you may want to consider a deferred compensation plan. A deferred compensation plan can reward you for past services in the company and act like a retirement plan. There is an agreement between you and the company to pay you a specified annual amount over a period of time. This creates a liability for the company which reduces its value and allows you to gift your business interest to the next generation without your family members having to come up with a significant amount of cash.

The deferred compensation payments are a contractual obligation and will reduce the amount that the next generation can take in compensation or distributions. They should pay you before starting to pay themselves higher-than-market salaries or make income distributions to themselves. It is important that you have an attorney and an accountant assist you in setting up a deferred compensation arrangement. You want to have it properly structured so that you can receive beneficial tax treatment. The IRS code, section 409A, deals with the tax treatment of deferred compensation.

It is not uncommon for the business owner to use a combination strategy, such as selling a percentage of the business and gifting the rest. This provides the owner with some proceeds to be used in retirement but makes it afford- able for the next generation. For any sale to family members, the IRS will want a business valuation from a qualified business valuator in order to make sure that the sale of the business wasn't a disguised gift. The IRS does not want business owners selling their business to their children for $1,000 when it is really worth $10 million. This action would save a significant amount of gift and estate tax and is not allowed by the IRS.

Whether you are implementing a gifting strategy or selling your business to family members, it is important that you have a basic understanding about estate and gift taxes.

Estate and Gift Taxes

Estate and gift tax rules are important issues to understand when consider- ing the gifting strategy. There is a complex set of IRS regulations governing all estates and gifts. I hear business owners say all the time: "Why can't I gift whatever I want whenever I want?" You can to your spouse or a charity, but no one else. This is because you could avoid any estate tax by simply gifting all of your assets to your children or someone else and having nothing in your estate when you die. Therefore, the IRS has volumes of rules and regulations that apply to estates and gifts. The following is a very simple overview of the estate and gift regulations:

- The assets in your estate or any gift that is transferred to your spouse or a charity is not subject to any gift or estate tax—regardless of the type of asset or the value of the asset.

- You can make a gift to anyone tax-free if the gift is below the annual gift exclusion level. That amount was increased to $14,000 in 2013. Any gift above the annual exclusion amount is subject to the gift tax. You will have to file a gift tax return (Form 709) for any gift made in excess of $14,000. If the amount of your gift exceeds what cur- rent legislation allows to be excluded, then you will owe a gift tax.

- The IRS allows a certain amount of your net worth to be excluded from estate and gift tax. Based on the tax legislation that was passed in January 2013, that amount is $5.25 million per individual and will subject to annually inflation adjustments. This means if you die with less than that year's exclusion, your heirs will not pay any federal estate tax (each state treatment of estate tax is different). You can also gift up to the gift exclusion level without paying any gift taxes. The estate and gift exclusion amounts are the same. The gift exclusion amount was lower than the estate exclusion amount in the years 2002–2009. The estate and gift exclusion level goes up and down based on legislation enacted by the US government. It is important that you keep informed on these changes and how much of your estate will be excluded from the estate tax.

- If your estate is above the amount that the IRS says can be excluded from estate tax, then you will have to pay estate tax. Beginning in 2013, the estate tax rate was 40%. So for every dollar in your estate (that does not go your spouse or charity) that is above the $5.25 million exclusion, your estate will owe the IRS 40 cents.

- With proper planning, you can combine the amount that is excluded from estate and gift tax with your spouse's exclusion. So in 2013, if you are married, you have the potential to exclude $10.5 million of your net worth from estate and gift tax.

The mechanics and intricacies of estate and gift planning are outside the scope of this book. It is much more complex than the quick summary I've provided. If you are interested in reading more about this from the IRS perspective, read the IRS Publication 950 at www.irs.gov/pub950.

The question you need to ask yourself is this: where will your family come up with the cash to pay any potential estate tax? A business may have a lot of value but not much liquidity. If you are in this situation, your family may need to sell the business in order to pay the estate tax. This can be avoided by either having enough life insurance on the business owner's life to pay the estate tax or by using an effective gifting strategy.

■ **Important**　You should meet with an experienced estate attorney to ensure that you understand the current estate and gift tax legislation and how it impacts your situation.

Implementing the Gifting Strategy

The best way to implement a gifting strategy is to do the opposite of the selling strategy. You will want to sell your business at its highest value and to gift your business when the value is depressed. This way, you will be able to gift a greater percentage of ownership with less tax impact when your business value is low. Also, it is best to implement this strategy when the tax laws are most favorable. Our valuation practice was swamped during the second half of 2012 because business owners were concerned that the estate tax exemption would decrease from $5 million to $1 million. Even though the tax law did not change dramatically, it was an opportune time to gift because the values of most businesses are depressed due to the lingering impact of the recession.

Since there are annual and lifetime gift tax exemption limits, a gifting strategy needs to be timed and planned. Most business owners like to gift several blocks of stock over a period of time. When a minority interest is gifted (less than a 50% interest), the value on a per share basis is lower because of the discounts for lack of control and marketability issues. How valuable is a 1% common stock interest in a closely held business? It has very little value if a company does not pay a significant amount of dividends because a minority shareholder has no power to change the operations of the business. Unlike a controlling shareholder, minority shareholders cannot set their salary or dividend policy, enter into an agreement to sell the business, or make any major decisions without the consent of other shareholders. You can transfer a significant amount of wealth by making several minority interest gifts.

When you make a gift of stock, it is important that you obtain a professionally prepared valuation that meets the IRS Revenue Ruling 59-60 requirements and attach the valuation report to the gift tax form, 709. When you file a gift tax return with a valuation report that meets the IRS standards, the statute of limitations begins and runs for three years after the return is filed. Once the statute of limitations lapses, you are protected from the IRS assessing additional estate or gift taxes.

Critical Issues for a Gifting Strategy

There are two critical concepts that you must embrace in order for a gifting strategy to be effective. The first is that you need to have enough wealth to support your retirement needs, and the second is that the next generation must be ready and able to take over the business.

That is why it is very important that you begin to implement your succession plan and gifting strategy early. You not only have to be concerned about building your own retirement, but you want to make sure that the next generation has the proper training and experience to be able to run the company. Family businesses have more minefields than a normal business. Not only do family business owners have to worry about what every other business owner worries about, but they also have family dynamics that impact the business. Many family businesses fail because the right people are not leading the company or because family conflict and other issues appear or transpire that are not related to general business items.

In order to deal with the family dynamics in a business and for the business to survive once you leave, it is very important that you consider forming a Family Business Council (FBC) and developing a family creed for the business.

An FBC, also known as a "family forum" or a "family assembly," is a formal meeting for the family members to discuss business and family issues. The meeting will address business, family, and succession issues as well as help you deal with them objectively. As the business passes from one generation to the next, it becomes crucial to establish a formal meeting. The FBC allows all family members to stay informed about business and succession issues. These meetings can help avoid potential conflicts that might arise among family members since everyone is on equal footing with the critical issues. The issues addressed at FBC meetings may include the following:

- Education of family members about their rights and responsibilities

- Approval of family employment and compensation policies

- Formalization of the succession-planning process

- Setting guidelines for family participation in ownership and management

- Other important family matters

As a general rule, the council should be open to all family members. However, some families prefer to set certain membership restrictions, such as minimum age limits and participation of in-laws. Involving children at the meeting will allow them to get a clear picture of what will be expected of them should they want to join the company. Although some FBCs are set up more formally than others, all should record minutes of the meetings to preserve a record for future decisions.

The family creed is a "rules of engagement" type of agreement among family members. Once it is developed, all family members who want to join the family business must sign the agreement. This is a critical document because expectations are expressed at the outset, making it easier to dismiss or discipline a family employee with a signed document that spells out the desired behavior. A sample family creed is located in Appendix D. Having an FBC and a family creed mitigates many issues that derail family businesses.

Gifting to a Charity

You can also gift an interest of your business to a charity and obtain a tax deduction. This rarely occurs and usually is done in conjunction with a sale of the business. Most charities have no interest in holding closely held company stock. They are willing to hold the stock if the company is making significant annual distributions or if the company will be sold soon. The donor of the gift will have a tax deduction and will be able to avoid capital gains on the sale of the shares gifted. If you gift an interest of your business to a charity, it must be at fair market value as determined by a qualified appraiser. The appraisal or valuation report that supports the gift must be attached to the taxpayer's federal income tax return along with Form 8283.

Retaining Your Business Interest

Today, more and more business owners are maintaining an interest in their business while walking away from their day-to-day duties. This option has grown significantly over the past few years and may be the most popular at this time. Why? The great recession and the low investment returns on alternative investments are the two main reasons.

The values of most businesses have decreased during the past few years. This is due to the lowered earnings as a result of the recent recession. Also, with the recent banking crisis, a buyer's ability to borrow money for the purchase of a business has decreased. Business owners who have placed their company on the market have been unpleasantly surprised by the offers they have received. When they do obtain a decent offer, they often determine that they cannot afford to sell. In the fall of 2012, the investment returns on safe investments were less than 2%. The return that owners can receive on their net sales proceeds (selling price less transaction costs and taxes) is nowhere near what they were earning from the business.

What should business owners do when they are ready to move on from the business but their financial needs cannot be met through alternative investments? What about owners who believe their business will be worth significantly more in the future but would like to do something else? What is the solution?

The solution is simply to retain your business and leave or greatly reduce your role. This means you need to either train or trust your existing management team to carry on without you or hire a professional management team. This step will allow you to continue receiving the economic benefits of owning the business while leaving (most of) the headaches to someone else.

Implementing the Retention Strategy

First, you have to determine if you can hand over the reins to someone else and limit your time at the office. Not all business owners can do this. Some will not be able to sleep while someone else is minding the store, while others can sail across the world and never have another thought about the business.

If this is your strategy, it is critical that you build a trusted management team. They need to be properly compensated in order to operate the business in a way that provides them with a very good living and keeps your dividends, salary, or other forms of compensation coming your way. This strategy will not work with incompetent management or with a management team that does not have a vested interest. It will be difficult to find employees who are willing to put in their blood, sweat, and tears for a meager salary and then watch the profits of the business being wired to you on some remote island.

There are a few good incentive plans that are available to management teams that will keep their interest and have them not feeling too badly about wiring you money. These are the most popular incentive plans:

- *Above-market wages:* One option is just to pay your successors very well. If they are getting paid much higher than they could elsewhere, it provides a great incentive to keep the business "cash machine" operating efficiently. This could be through higher salaries or by a contractual bonus arrangement based on their performance and the profits of the company. I have seen many plans that provide management with a certain percentage of the pretax profits.

- *Stock ownership:* Providing key managers with stock ownership may appear to be a way to keep your key executives; however, I don't like this strategy. It may not provide the reward they want and can cause problems if you need to terminate an employee who owns stock. Minority shareholders do have legal rights. If an employee is fired, not only can he file a lawsuit for wrongful termination, but he can also file a lawsuit as an oppressed minority shareholder. As discussed previously, a minority interest in a company does not provide the owner with any financial benefits. I do not recommend this option unless the management team will be the ultimate buyers of your stock.

- *Phantom stock plan:* This is pretend stock, but it can be better than real stock. The owner and the management team come to an agreement on the value of the company (hopefully with the assistance of a business valuator) at the time the phantom plan is established. The management team is compensated by receiving a specified percentage of the increase of value in the company over time while they are employed. Sometimes this is used when owners want to sell their business down the road and want the management team to work very hard to obtain a higher price. I like phantom stock plans because they are easy to draft and understand and can be very effective.

- *Future buy-out at a prearranged price:* This is an agreement between the business owner and the management team. The management team has the right to buy out the business at a price that is predetermined. The prearranged price is important since you don't want to disincentivize the management team in making the company more valuable. Since they know that they will own the business in the future, they will have an owner and not an employee mindset while managing the company. This is effective when the owner only needs to retain the business for a couple of years. It is not very effective if management does not know when they will be owners or if their ownership is too far into the future.

Critical Issues for a Retention Strategy

You can retain the business for a significant period of time if you have the right management team with the proper incentive plan. However, at some point, you will no longer own the business. It may be on your terms, or it may be due to something out of your control.

In many cases, the existing management team is the best exit strategy since they know the business but they may not want it or be able to afford it. It is critical that you have an alternative exit strategy mapped out with the retention strategy. This is true even if your plan is to keep the business for 20 years. It is also important that you determine what happens to your business if you die and document your wishes in your estate plan.

The other critical issue is determining how much involvement you will have with the business. One suggestion is to formalize your corporate structure and governance before stepping out of the day-to-day operations. This will include having regular board of director meetings and relying more on outside advisors. If you're not very active in the business, I recommend that you have an annual audit and quarterly board meetings where the management team discusses the quarter results and the prospect for the future.

Retention Strategy Example

The following example will be helpful in understanding the economic impact of the retention strategy. Let's assume that the annual pretax earnings of your business is $800,000. You want to leave the business and enjoy life, but it is not the right time to sell your business. In order to make this happen, you hire someone to run the company and have additional accounting and other fees to manage the business. The additional cost of doing this is $200,000 a year. On a go-forward basis, the business is now making $600,000 a year before taxes. Let's assume a 33% tax rate and that all the after-tax profits can be distributed to you because the company has a strong balance sheet and can finance future capital expenditures.

Your annual distribution from the business would be $400,000, and this is significantly higher than what your annual earnings would be on the after-tax proceeds from selling your business reinvested at today's low interest rates.

You also would receive proceeds from the sale of the company in the future. In this example, you estimate that you can sell your business at $5 million 10 years from now and that your after-tax proceeds will be $3.5 million. The present value of the 10 years of annual distributions and the cash proceeds from selling the company in 10 years is $3.8 million (assuming a 10% discount rate). The following is a summary of this calculation:

Annual Pretax Earnings	$	800,000
Additional Expenses to Manage		(200,000)
Revised Pretax Earnings		600,000
Income Taxes		(200,000)
Your Annual Distribution	$	400,000
Present Value of Distributions over 10 Years		2,458,000
Present Value of Proceeds from Sale in 10 Years		1,349,000
Present Value of Retention Strategy	$	3,807,000

You can see that this is an economically viable option for many business owners. It can only be used if you can leave the business and trust someone else running your company. But what if you can't do that and you cannot sell your business? Liquidation is an option, and there is a right way and a wrong way to implement this strategy.

Liquidating Your Business Interest

Liquidation is the exit strategy that is the easiest to understand and implement. However, it produces the lowest amount of proceeds (except for a gift) to the owner compared with the other exit strategies. Most businesses are worth more than the sum parts of receivables, inventory, and equipment. With liquidation, the owner usually does not receive anything for the value of the intangible assets (e.g., the goodwill that you have with your customers). Liquidation involves reducing your business to its component parts. You sell off individual assets and then pay off all your obligations and walk away.

Why would anyone decide on this exit strategy? Usually, it is the exit strategy of last resort. The owner may have tried to sell the business over time but could not reach an agreement with any buyer. The choice for those who want to sell their business but can't is to either retain the business or liquidate it.

The owner may choose to liquidate rather than to retain the business because of one of the following conditions:

- The business is losing money or barely breaking even.

- The owner or a family member has health issues.

- The owner is burnt out and wants to retire or do something else.

- The owner can make more money doing something else.

In very rare cases, an orderly liquidation can bring in more proceeds than a sale of the business. This is particularly true for a small retail business. The "going out of business sale" is conducted by outside professionals that will bring in other inventory to sell. There are instances that I have seen where the business owners have made more money in a "going out of business sale" than by selling their business. It happens, but it is rare.

The other situation when someone can make more on a liquidation than keeping the business is when an asset owned by the business is more valuable than the earnings stream of the business. An example of this is real estate. If the real estate owned by the business becomes valuable to someone else (i.e., mineral rights, location premium to another business, or eminent domain) and the company is willing to pay a significant premium for the real estate, the owner may want to sell the real estate and liquidate the rest of the business.

Sometimes, the liquidation strategy is forced upon the business owner. This can occur due to improper planning, business conditions, or unfortunate events. The reasons for "forced" liquidation include the following:

- The owner dies with no exit strategy or succession plan.

- A bank or other creditor forces the business to liquidate.

- The company loses a lawsuit and has no insurance to pay the judgment.

- The company violates a governmental regulation (IRS, Department of Labor (DOL), or EPA) and is unable to solve the issue and/or cannot pay the associated fine.

Implementing the Liquidation Strategy

There are two ways to implement a liquidation exit strategy: through an orderly liquidation or through a forced liquidation.

The orderly liquidation occurs over a period of time and should be very intentional. You will want to carefully plan the liquidation and have at least 6 to

12 months to implement it. Some assets lose significant value if they have to be sold in a short time period. This includes inventory, machinery and equipment, and real estate. If your exit strategy is liquidation, make sure that you time it so that you don't have any major obligations left once the liquidation is complete. You don't want to liquidate your business and still be paying rent on your building lease. Sometimes this cannot be helped. I have seen cases where the business owner was better off eating the rent than continuing the business operations. If you are losing $100,000 a year and your rent is $50,000 a year, you are better off shutting down the business and absorbing the rent and finding a job.

Hire a professional to sell your real estate and equipment and provide this professional with enough advance notice so that you can get the best price. Sell as much of your inventory as you can through your normal business processes.

The key to an orderly liquidation is planning. Proper planning and allowing enough time to obtain the best price for your assets will maximize your return. The tax consequence of a liquidation will depend on whether you sell your assets at a price higher than your original cost less the amount that has been depreciated (tax basis).

There are limited strategies for a forced liquidation. If it is due to creditor issues, bankruptcy, or a lawsuit, your best strategy is to obtain the services of a competent, experienced attorney. When you reach this point, your goal is to simply retain as much value as possible and to limit your personal liability exposure.

Summary

Paul Simon sang that there are "50 ways to leave your lover." There are many more ways to leave a lover than a business, but leaving a business successfully will take much more planning and forethought than leaving a lover.

The most popular strategy and most lucrative is the selling strategy. However, this is not the best strategy if you want your kids to take over the reins someday. If that is the case, a gifting strategy should be considered. If your plans are to either gift or sell the business, you must execute a well thought-out plan to be successful.

The recent recession and bank failures have made selling your business much harder. Because of these conditions, some owners have decided to retain their business for a few more years. Some are working longer than expected and waiting for the right time to sell. Others have decided to hire a professional management team and scale back their responsibilities and time at their business.

This is a better alternative than selling the business, paying taxes, and reinvesting the proceeds in an investment that produces very low returns.

The least popular option and the one that will provide you with the lowest amount of money is the liquidation strategy. This is usually the option of last resort.

In the next chapter, we go through a few scenarios to assist you in determining which exit strategy may be the best fit for your situation. We will also discuss the process you need to go through to provide you with the best chance of exiting your business on your terms.

Know Your Exit Strategy

No More Procrastination

Determining your exit strategy and ultimate succession plan is a challenging endeavor. This is a once-in-a-lifetime decision. It is more difficult for second and third generation businesses. It becomes very complicated and cumbersome for a multigenerational business that has multiple owners.

Recently, I was engaged by a second-generation business to develop an exit strategy and succession plan. The patriarch established the business 40 years ago and about 10 years ago gifted the business to his two sons and daughter. The company is owned equally by three children whose ages are between 45 and 60. During our initial meeting, the oldest brother announced that he planned to leave the company in five years. He stated that he will gift his stock to his kids (who work in the business) and continue to collect his salary once he retires. The youngest brother wanted to sell the business in five years and have all the brothers leave at the same time. The daughter thought the best plan was to franchise the operations and then collect royalties to fund their retirement.

What is the right answer here? How can the three siblings get on the same page when there is such diversity in their opinions? These were the questions I asked myself after our initial meeting. A year and four meetings later, they have selected their exit strategy and there is a consensus among the siblings. We are now working on a plan to execute the exit strategy, something that will be up to them to do.

I did not gain clarity on their plan until I performed an analysis on each exit strategy and held three more meetings to discuss the various options. This analysis showed the impact of each exit strategy on the company's future operations and their individual retirements. Once the implications of their desired options were on paper, it was easier to make a decision. For instance, the brother who desired to sell the business in five years realized that the proceeds he would receive from selling would not be enough to allow him to retire at age 50.

I believe the shareholders now realize that their initial thoughts about exiting the business were a little naïve. The process was going to be more difficult than any of them expected. The honest and uncomfortable quarterly sessions have been invaluable and a direction has been set. There is still a long way to go, and I hope that there will be no major roadblocks that will cause their plans to change. But by addressing exit strategies now, they will have options if the unexpected comes up.

The purpose of this chapter is to assist you in determining which exit strategy best fits your situation. Once you determine your exit strategy, you can make specific plans to accomplish your chosen strategy.

■ **Important**   Determining your exit strategy and succession plan is slow work that cannot be hurried, but it is also urgent work that cannot be put off.

The Procrustean Bed

Procrustes was a deceitful character from Greek mythology. He enticed weary travelers to stay at his house with a pleasant meal and a night's rest. He would tell about his "magical bed" that would be a perfect fit for travelers no matter how tall or short they were.

He was right about the bed being a perfect fit. However, the travelers were sorry that they slept on his magical bed. If they were too long for the bed, he chopped their feet off. And if they were too short for the bed, he would stretch the guests until they were the same length as the bed. It was truly a "one size fits all" bed.

A Procrustean solution is therefore the practice of tailoring complex issues into a "one size fits all" plan. There are consultants, advisors, and books that will either sell you on their preconceived notion of what your exit strategy should be or use a "one size fits all" packaged solution. I hope you will avoid a Procrustean solution for your exit strategy and succession plan.

The personal nature and complexity of your situation cannot be solved by a "canned program" or by looking only at one strategy. It is very important that you fully understand all of your options, take a deliberate approach to selecting your exit strategy, and answer the following question:

■ **How do you leave the business on *your* terms?**

Stop the procrastination and schedule some time on your calendar to start the process. One day, you will leave your business. Act now to make sure it is on your terms. The sooner you plan your exit, the more options you will have.

What Is the Next Step?

Maybe it is clear to you how you will exit your business. If so, have you prepared an analysis of what your after-tax proceeds will be from your current exit strategy? Does this amount, along with your other assets, provide you with the retirement you desire? This analysis will provide you with a litmus test of how close you are to achieving your financial goals under your current exit strategy. After seeing how your plans play out on paper, you may choose a different strategy or become more focused on increasing the value of your business.

What if you don't know your exit strategy? How can you make a decision in this important area? What can you do today to start the process that allows you to exit your business on your terms?

There is no Procrustean solution to determine your best exit strategy. It will take time and hard work to make sure you have the right plan. If you take the following steps during the next 12 to 18 months, you will be closer to having a well-defined exit strategy and succession plan:

- Study the various exit strategies and understand the advantages and disadvantages of each strategy as they apply to your situation.

- Estimate the net after-tax proceeds that will you will obtain from each exit strategy.

- Spend time reflecting on how your decision about your exit will impact the future of your family and the employees of your company.

- Develop plans on how you will spend your time once you leave your business. Is this attractive to you?

- Have a dialog with family members, key employees, and advisors about your preferred exit strategy and how it will impact them.

- Select the strategy that best meets your personal, financial, and family goals.

Which Strategy for Your Situation?

To point you in the right direction and narrow down some of your options, I am going to provide you with information on which exit strategy works best in various situations. I have talked about each of these strategies, but it may be beneficial for you to look at the various exit strategies presented in a different order. The following are the exit strategies listed in the order of providing the highest amount of after-tax proceeds immediately after you exit your business:

- Selling to a synergistic buyer

- Selling to an ESOP

- Selling to a financial buyer

- Selling to an insider (family member or employee)

- Retaining the business after your exit

- Liquidating the business

- Gifting your stock in the business

Selling to a Synergistic Buyer

As we have explained earlier, this option will provide you with the highest price. However, the number of synergistic buyers is limited, and this option is not available to all business owners. You will want to consider selling to a synergistic buyer if you are in one of the following situations:

- *Obtaining the highest price is most important to you*: Many start a business to become rich. This strategy will provide the highest selling price for you. If you are concerned about your legacy or the future of your employees, then another option may be better.

- *You have a retirement shortfall*: You may not like the idea of selling to a competitor or other synergistic buyer, but it may be the only way to meet your retirement needs.

- *The sell would provide a windfall that secures your family for life*: I have been involved in deals where the business owner obtains tens of millions of dollars. They are able to provide financial security for their entire family for life and support charities they love. You may want your children to take your business, but it is hard to pass up an offer that secures your children's financial future and allows them to pursue other endeavors.

Selling to an ESOP

If you sell your stock to an ESOP, it will be at a lower price than selling it to a synergistic buyer. However, you could end up with more after-tax proceeds. This is because you will have the opportunity to defer paying taxes from the gain of the sale of your stock (at least a 30% interest) to an ESOP. In order for this to happen, the proceeds must be reinvested in certain domestic investments (see IRS section 1042 for specifics). With proper estate planning, the deferral can become permanent and the gain from your business is tax-free. ESOPs are not easy to establish and can be costly to maintain. They are only possible if you have a strong management team that is able to operate your business once you leave. You will want to consider selling your stock to an ESOP if you are in one of the following situations:

- *You desire to preserve the culture once you leave:* This is a good option if you want to preserve both jobs and the culture you created. Outside buyers will run the business as they wish and may make changes you will not like. By selling it to your employees, it is more likely that your philosophy and legacy will continue than if you sell it to outsiders.

- *Your retirement needs are met:* If you do not need the proceeds from the sale of your business to fund your retirement or other lifestyle needs, then you should consider an ESOP. With proper planning, you may be able to pass the funds you receive from the sale of the business to your heirs tax-free.

- *There is a limited market for your business:* Some business owners sell their business to an ESOP after exhausting the other options. This is not the best reason to sell to an ESOP.

Selling to a Financial Buyer

Most business transactions are to a financial buyer that is not part of the business. There is a large universe of financial buyers, but they are hard to identify. Financial buyers can range from private equity groups to local corporate executives who have lost their jobs. They may be experienced buyers or complete novices. You will want to consider this option when the following apply to your situation:

- *A synergistic buyer is not available*: If you cannot attract a synergistic buyer and do not want to pursue an ESOP, then this option will provide you with the highest price. This is particularly true if there is competition among financial buyers for your business.

- *You do not want a synergistic buyer*: You may wish to pre-serve your culture and maintain jobs, but selling to family members or employees is not an option. Try to locate a financial buyer that has similar values and philosophy. If this is important to you, spend considerable amount of time with the buyer to make sure he or she is the right person to continue your legacy once you leave.

Selling to an Insider

Selling to your children or other family members and employees will provide you with the lowest amount of cash at closing compared with the other selling options. Most of the time, your children and employees do not have the financial resources needed to buy a business. Therefore, the amount of cash received at closing will be less than other options and you will have to finance a large part of the purchase price. Consider this strategy if the following is important to you:

- *Your children own the business but not as a gift*: Some parents want their kids to buy the business as a matter of principle. This could be a moral or fairness issue. They may believe it is better for their children's character that they have to buy the business with their own resources. Also, some business owners have a difficult time gifting stock to children who work in the business and not making similar value gifts to children outside the business.

- *You want an insider to own the business, but you do not have enough for your retirement*: Some parents sell the business to their children because they need the sale proceeds to retire. It is not a character or fairness issue but a financial one. Consider this option if you want an insider to own the business, but you need more resources to retire. In some situations, parents use a combination gift-and-sell strategy to make it more affordable.

- *You would like to continue to show up to work*: If you sell the business to insiders, they may let you keep the keys to the front door and even ask you for your advice. When you sell it to an unrelated party, the new owners probably will make you turn in your keys, shake your hand, and wish you the best of luck.

Retaining the Business After Your Exit

This is an attractive option if you want to scale back and let someone else handle the daily headaches of running a business. In the long run, this exit strategy may provide you with the largest economic return. You should only select this option if you can trust your management team to operate the business effectively while you are away. You also need to have the ability to be away from the business and sleep at night. You should consider this strategy if these situations apply:

- *You would like to exit the business, but it is not the right time to sell*: You may be ready to exit, but you believe that your business is worth more than your current offers. If you think you can receive a significantly higher price in the future, this may be your best strategy.

- *Receiving annual distributions is attractive*: You may decide that you can obtain a greater economic return by keeping your business and letting someone else run it. The annual distributions that you receive will probably be much higher than the amount you will receive after selling your business and investing in alternative investments. If you believe that the business can operate without your daily presence, this may be your best economic option.

Liquidating the Business

Other than giving your business away, this option provides you with the lowest economic return. These are a few reasons why someone may choose this strategy:

- *Your business is not sellable*: There are certain types of businesses that cannot be sold due to the personal nature of the business. For example, an artist who has a unique skill may not be able to sell his business. This can be true for a brain surgeon or cabinetmaker. If you are in this situation, the best thing you can do is to earn as much as you can and invest as much as possible into your retirement plan.

- *Your business is worth more dead than alive*: There are some circumstances where the owner is better off liquidating the business. If your business is losing money or just breaking even, you may want to consider an orderly liquidation.

- *You don't care*: If you simply do not care what happens to your business or how much your heirs receive once you die, then this is the strategy for you. It is not one I recommend.

Gifting Your Stock in the Business

This is the ideal strategy if you want your legacy to continue and your children are prepared to take over the business. Of course you will not receive any economic benefit from gifting your business, but a successful implementation of this strategy can make you rich in other ways. It takes a great deal of discipline and effort to leave your business to your children and ensure that the business thrives once you leave. It is a source of great satisfaction to the business owner when this is accomplished.

You will want to consider this strategy if you have properly funded your retirement and believe that your children have the skills and resources to run the business.

■ **Important**   A successful exit from your business does not end once you have chosen your exit strategy. After selecting your exit strategy, develop or update your strategic and succession plan to give you the best chance of exiting on your terms.

Rebelle Handbags

As a further assistance in determining your exit strategy, I will walk you through an example. Let me introduce you to Elle, the business owner of a company called Rebelle Handbags.

Elle is 56 years old. She established the business when she was 40 years old. The company sells designer handbags to high-end customers. Close to 40% of total revenues come from sales to two large department stores. Elle has been working hard to increase web-based sales, which is currently 20% of total revenues. Elle has two children, and her oldest daughter works in the business as the lead designer.

Elle would like to exit her business within five years. Her lifetime dream is to serve orphans in a foreign land, and she would like to get started on this before she is too old to travel. To accomplish her dream, she will have to leave the United States for months at a time. She does not want to be bothered with business issues while she is gone. Excluding the business, Elle's net worth is $1.5 million. This includes $1 million in retirement savings and $500,000 of other investments. Her current compensation from the business is $300,000 a year. With the assistance of a financial planner, she has determined that she needs to have $150,000 a year in annual earnings once she retires.

She has started the process of determining her exit strategy. Elle does not know if her daughter has the business savvy to run the business and doubts she can afford to gift the company to her. Every year, one of her competitors calls her about selling the business.

She hired a valuation expert to provide a valuation of her business based on an investment value (synergistic buyer) and fair market value (financial buyer). She also requested an analysis of what her proceeds will be from each exit strategy and how each strategy will impact her future retirement. She expects to earn a 4% return on her retirement savings and will start to withdraw the interest income from her principal when she sells the business and after she is age 59 1/2. She also expects to earn 4% from the net proceeds she receives from the sale of the business. It is important to her to be able to live off the interest and dividends and not have to touch any of her investment principal.

The valuation expert determined that she could sell her business to a synergistic buyer for $2.5 million and to a financial buyer for $2 million. Can she retire today and begin her mission work? Here is a summary of the valuation expert's findings:

	Synergistic Buyer	Financial Buyer	Liquidate	Retain	Gift
Gross proceeds from business exit	$ 2,500,000	$ 2,000,000	$ 1,000,000	$ -	$ -
Transaction costs and taxes	(750,000)	(600,000)	(100,000)	-	-
Proceeds after exiting business	$ 1,750,000	$ 1,400,000	$ 900,000	$ -	$ -
Investment income from business exit	70,000	56,000	36,000	250,000	-
Investment Income from retirement funds	40,000	40,000	40,000	40,000	40,000
Investment income after exiting business	$ 110,000	$ 96,000	$ 76,000	$ 290,000	$ 40,000
Net worth after executing exit strategy	$ 3,250,000	$ 2,900,000	$ 2,400,000	$ 2,900,000	$ 1,500,000

Based on this analysis, it is clear that the gifting strategy will not work, and she is going to take the proper steps to make sure that the liquidation strategy is never used. The retention strategy is appealing from the income level, but she is concerned that she does not have a strong enough management team to maintain the cash flow once she is gone. Also, since she plans to be out of the country for months at a time, this option does not appeal to her. At this point, she is down to either selling to a synergistic or financial buyer. Even if she sold to a synergistic buyer, the proceeds that she would receive is not enough to provide her with $150,000 a year. She either has to live on less or grow the value of her business.

Armed with this information, she has a meeting with her financial advisor. They decide that she can retire when her net worth is in the $4.5 million range. She wants to know the selling price that is required in order for her to achieve a $4.5 million net worth. She would love to sell the business to someone who will retain all her employees, but this will not prevent her from selling to the highest bidder to reach her goals.

She realizes now that it will be at least three years before she can sell her business, but she does not want it to be more than five years. During the next three years, she feels like she can increase her retirement savings and believes her annual earnings from her retirement savings can be increased to $50,000 a year. During the next three years Elle expects to increase the value of her retirement and other investments to $2 million.

The following analysis was prepared to show her what the selling price of the company needs to be to meet her goals:

	Synergistic Buyer	Financial Buyer
Gross proceeds from sale	$ 4,200,000	$ 3,500,000
Transaction costs and taxes	(1,260,000)	(1,050,000)
Proceeds after exiting business	$ 2,940,000	$ 2,450,000
Investment income from sale proceeds	117,600	98,000
Investment Income from retirement funds	50,000	50,000
Investment income after exiting business	$ 167,600	$ 148,000
Net worth after executing exit strategy	$ 4,940,000	$ 4,450,000

Now she has a target to shoot for and is committed to being as aggressive as possible in growing the value of the business. If she can sell her business for $3.5 million, she is ready to "cash in her chips."

In order to retire at the lifestyle she wants, Elle will need to increase the value of her business significantly. Can she do this? The answer is "no" if she chooses to be passive and does not develop a plan to grow the value of her business. The answer may be "yes" with the right plan and proper execution of the plan. In the next chapter, I will discuss how to develop plans to grow the value of your business and show you Elle's plan to achieve her goal.

Summary

There is no Procrustean solution in determining your exit strategy. You need to understand all of the available options and perform an analysis to determine which exit strategy best matches your personal goals.

The most important step you need to take today is to start the process. Schedule a day or two each quarter to work on your exit strategy and succession plan. Once you choose your exit strategy, you need to develop a plan of action to make sure you are able to exit on your terms.

Time for Action

Your Plan to Retire Rich

It is the beginning of a new year, and I am noticing new faces at the gym. They are easy to spot. They are the ones with new workout clothes, and the trainer is showing them how to properly operate each machine. Their intentions are good, but few of them will succeed. Within a few months, most will never walk into the gym again.

There have been many times when I have made the New Year's resolution that I will get into the best shape of my life. I read the latest fitness books, made vows to eat healthy, and once even joined a weight-loss contest to hold myself accountable. One year, I hired a personal trainer. She provided me with precise measurements of my weight, body fat percentage, waist size, and other vital measurements. She laid out a detailed workout schedule and eating plan. At that time, I had all the knowledge and resources needed to get into the best shape of my life. Did I do it? No. Why not? It was because I was missing a few critical items to make my plan a success. I did not have the right motivation nor did I make it a priority in my life.

Recently, I have had better success in my journey of physical fitness. I have done this with fewer resources (I no longer have a personal trainer), and I am not spending hours reading about the latest fitness craze. What has changed? It is my motivation and the fact that I now make physical fitness a top priority.

My motivation and ability to stick with the plan came from stepping back and envisioning what my life would look like 5, 10, or 20 years from now if I kept on living an unhealthy lifestyle. Also, I did not like the results of my latest physical, and I did not have the energy for the really important things in my life. Will my newfound passion for working out and eating healthy guarantee that I will live a long happy life and achieve my personal goals? Of course not. There are no guarantees about our future no matter what we do. However, I will have a much greater chance of fulfilling my goals with a healthy lifestyle than I would if I completely ignored my health.

The journey of developing a healthy lifestyle is similar to the journey of making your business more valuable. You may know exactly what your business is worth and know exactly what you need to do to make it more valuable. You may have even hired a business coach to push you along. However, you need more than knowledge to grow the value of your business and exit your business on your terms. I did not become healthier because I learned about personal fitness, joined a gym, and developed a fitness plan. Changes happened to my health when I started to execute my plan.

Developing a plan to grow the value of your business is a critical step in achieving greater personal wealth. The only way it will succeed is if you have the right motivation and if you make growing the value of your business a priority.

In the first chapter, I discussed Stephen Covey's *The 7 Habits of Highly Effective People*. In order to achieve your goals, it is important to embrace the concepts of *Beginning with the End in Mind* and *Putting First Things First*. These two concepts will allow you to be focused on seeing your plan through when the daily urgent business and personal issues start to overwhelm you and scream for your attention.

You can develop the greatest plan in the world, have the right motivation, and work hard on the execution of your plan and not achieve your goals. The business world is too complex and random for you to completely control your destiny. However, I do know that you will retire with greater riches by working diligently on a plan to grow the value of your business than you would if you left everything to chance.

Throughout the book, I have discussed the importance of having an investment mindset toward your business. Business owners with this mindset will be more successful in meeting their personal wealth goals than typical business owners. The same goes for individual investors. With stocks and bonds, you look for ways to improve your investment returns and so should you with your business investment. You know that there is a big difference in the future value of your investments when you are able to increase the annual return from 5% to 10% over a long period of time.

How do you create a plan to maximize the investment return on your business investment? The key is to treat your business like any other investment. This means having a plan to grow your investment and actively working that plan. In this chapter, I will discuss what should be included in a plan to grow the value of your business and how to execute your plan.

Tip Begin with the end in mind and determine what retiring rich means to you. For some, it is retiring with millions of dollars, and for others it is successfully transferring the business to their kids. Keep your goal in front of you so that you can focus on the important issues and not be consumed by the urgent issues.

Critical Items to Your Plan's Success

Too many plans (strategic and growth plans) are sitting in the top drawer of the business owner's desk collecting dust. Many of these plans have a lot of nice-looking color graphs and slick photos that would impress anyone. The owner spent a significant amount of time and money in developing the plan. But it is completely worthless since it is gathering dust. How do you make sure all of your hard work and money spent on the planning process will be worth the effort? I believe that there are three critical concepts that you need to embrace in order to make your plan a success.

The first concept is setting the right "tone from the top." You need to communicate that the execution of the plan is very important to you and that you are allocating a significant amount of time and resources to accomplish the plan. Your employees will see that you are serious about this and know that they will be held accountable for their contribution to the plan. If it is not important to you, it will not be important to others.

The second concept is selecting the right people for your team. It can be a very lonely position being a business owner, and some owners slip into silo thinking and are not open to outside ideas. We all have blind spots and self-serving biases that lead us down the wrong path. It is important that you have members of your team (advisors and employees) that can provide you with candor and are not afraid to challenge you. You want team members that can push and exhort each other to obtain the best result.

The third concept is to make sure that your plan is achievable and tailored to your situation and culture. The reason why so many plans collect dust is because they are either too ambitious or too theoretical. I remember seeing a plan that had over 100 goals and action items with some impressive words that I did not understand. The plan did not accomplish much. The employees knew from day one that those goals and action items could not be accomplished. Make sure that all those involved understand what is being asked of them and that they believe that they can perform their assigned tasks in the time frame requested.

■ **Important**   Develop a plan that includes honest input from your key employees and advisors. Also make sure it is easy to understand and achievable. Your time and resources are too valuable to waste on a plan that will not work for you and all involved.

What to Include in Your Plan

There is not much published about how to develop a specific plan to grow the value of your business investment. You may be able to look at one of the many strategic planning books to assist you in creating a plan to grow the value of your business. You need to tailor that advice to focus on growing your business value and try not to get too bogged down by the process or the terminology that is used in these books. Many authors make the strategic planning process too complex. In my opinion, a simple straightforward plan works the best.

The following are the steps that I suggest you take in developing and executing a plan to grow the value of your business:

- Know the current value of your business.

- Set a growth goal for your business value.

- Identify ways you can increase the value of your business from the following valuation drivers:

  - Increasing your sustainable future cash flow

  - Lowering your business risks

  - Increasing your growth prospects

- Select goals that are attainable and measurable and then develop strategies and action plans to achieve those goals.

- Assign responsibilities and hold people accountable.

- Have quarterly meetings to monitor the progress.

- Reassess when necessary.

We have discussed at length the importance of having a business valuation and how it is not possible to start your growth plan without a realistic view of what your business is worth. Once you have determined the value, it is important to set a growth goal. You may set an annual percentage increase-in-value goal or an amount that you want your business to be worth at the end of a certain time period. Whatever method you choose, it is important to have a target set for your future business value.

Once you know the value of your business and set a target for its future value, the next step is to identify ways to increase the value of your business. The approach that I like best is to spend a day with the business owner and key employees away from their facility and discuss the critical areas that are impacting the value of the business. I rank in order the items that have the biggest impact on value and have them rank in order the items they feel that they can influence the most. This exercise results in a consensus on what items the team should focus on during the next few months and years to increase the value of the business.

The next step is to select a few specific goals (three to six) that the management team will concentrate on to make the business more valuable. I like to make sure that there is a consensus on the selected goals and that these goals can be achieved and progress measured. Having a plan and stated goals is great, but it is actually the easy part. It is like reading a book about fitness, buying the gym membership, and hiring the personal trainer. Without showing up and working out, you will not reach your physical goals. The same goes for your plan to grow the value of your business. The right execution plan is critical.

For each goal, select a champion who will be responsible for the achievement of that goal. This person's job is to develop the right strategies and actions to accomplish the goal. You need to have in place the right people who have the time and resources to get the job done. To help ensure the plan continues on course, hold quarterly meetings that focus only on the progress being made in increasing the value of the business. These meetings offer an opportunity to remind everyone what the plan entails and how each person contributes to the success of the plan.

There will be a time when it becomes evident that a particular goal or champion for that goal needs to be changed. Reassess and step back. Also, look at your value growth plan on an annual basis or when a major event takes place. Your plan is a living, fluid document and reassessing it provides you with the opportunity to change the goal, tactics, or personnel if the situation warrants.

Tip Have your quarterly meetings to discuss the progress of your plan at an offsite location. Don't allow your team to be distracted by the day-to-day issues when discussing the plan to grow the value of your business.

Elle's Plan to Double Her Business Value

If you remember from the last chapter, Elle wants to exit her business during the next three to five years to fulfill her lifelong dream of serving orphans in a foreign land. She has determined that her best exit strategy is to sell her business. She is undecided as to whether it will be to a synergistic or financial buyer. In order for her to be able to live her dream retirement, she has decided to develop a plan to grow the value of her business over the next three to five years. Elle is motivated to improve the value of her business. But what specific steps does she need to take in order to accomplish her goal?

The first step Elle takes is to set a target growth rate for her business. Her goal is to increase the value of her business by 15% per year over the next five years. If she is able to accomplish this goal, the value of Rebelle Handbags will double and she will have more than enough to meet her stated financial goals.

After setting her goal, she and her management team go to a retreat center to focus on developing a plan to increase the value of the company. She already knows from the valuation process the areas that have impacted the value of her business. At the start of her planning retreat, she has the valuation consultant go over the issues that had the biggest negative impact on the value of the business. The consultant told the team that with improvement in the following items, the value of Rebelle Handbags would increase dramatically:

- The reliance on two customers for 40% of revenues made the business risky from an outsider's perspective.

- Customers are buying illegal knockoffs that are sold on the Internet. The value of the business was negatively impacted two ways. First, cash flow is lower from the diverted sales. Second, the risk factor was increased because of the unknown future impact that the sale of knockoffs will have on the business.

- There is too much reliance on Elle in the operations of the business. Any buyer would be concerned about the impact her exit would have on future operations.

- The five-year historical annual growth rate is just less than 2%, and the forecasted growth rate is in a similar range. This is lower than the forecasted growth of the general economy and the industry.

- The company's gross margin percentage was lower than others in the industry and declining.

- The operating expenses seemed high for the size of the business and were increasing.

- Earnings have been inconsistent and are not predictable.

- The company relies on one supplier for all handbag materials.

Elle had the valuation consultant provide her with what the value of her business would be if all these issues were rectified. She was in shock; her value would be lot more than her goal of doubling the value—she could triple or quadruple the value over time. She thought to herself, "It is time to go to work!"

After two days of focused attention, Elle and her management team decided to focus on these six goals to increase the value of her business:

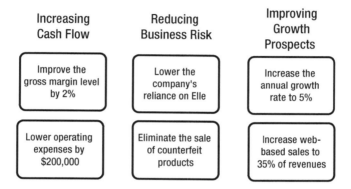

Elle is excited and motivated after developing these goals, and now she knows it is important to start attacking each of them. The group prioritized each goal and began to discuss specific strategies and action plans needed to achieve each goal. Elle is just one person, and she knows it will be a team effort in order for the plan to be successful. During the retreat, she selected a champion for each goal and provided due dates for the initial strategy development and the expected date when the goal would be implemented. Here is a table of the stated goals, who is responsible, and the projected due dates:

Goal to Increase Value	Goal Champion	Initial Strategy Development	Implementation Date
Reduction of operating expenses	Chief Financial Officer	3/31/2013	6/30/2013
Increase gross margin by 2%	Chief Financial Officer	6/30/2013	12/31/2013
Protection from counterfeits	Corporate Lawyer	6/30/2013	12/31/2013
Accelerate web-based revenues	Vice President of Sales	12/31/2013	6/30/2014
Hire a chief operating officer (COO)	Elle & Executive Search Firm	3/31/2014	9/30/2014
Increase sales growth to 5%	Vice President of Sales	6/30/2014	12/31/2014

The specific strategies and action plans developed for each goal will be multi-fold. For example, regarding the goal of increasing the gross margin by 2%, the CFO may hire a lean consultant to provide suggestions on gaining production efficiencies. He may also look for a more cost-effective supplier of the materials. It is his job to determine the proper strategy and actions to take to accomplish the goal.

Some of the goals will be much easier to accomplish than others. Finding a replacement for Elle may be as simple as hiring a skilled executive search firm. Developing strategies to increase the annual revenue growth to 5%, on the other hand, will be much more challenging.

A plan is only as good as the follow-up. Elle decides that the team will meet offsite for the entire day once a quarter. At that meeting, team members will provide an update on the progress they made on their part of the plan and obtain honest feedback from others about the progress made. Elle will decide on which parts of the plan are progressing well and which ones are not. She can then determine whether to change some of the goals or change who is responsible for making the goal a reality.

What Is Success?

The subtitle of this book is "An Owner's Guide to Retiring Rich." The definition of retiring rich has a different meaning for each business owner. For Elle, it meant using the resources from selling her business to serve orphans in a foreign land. For you, it may mean making millions of dollars or seeing your son or daughter successfully running a business that you started on a shoestring budget. Whatever your definition of riches is, go after it with sense of purpose and a plan. I love this quote from Napoleon Hill, the author of *Think and Grow Rich*, which has sold over 70 million copies:

> There is one quality which one must possess to win, and that is definiteness of purpose, the knowledge of what one wants, and a burning desire to possess it.

There is no guarantee that you will be successful and be able to retire rich by reading this book and starting to treat your business like an investment. However, you will end up richer by treating your company like an investment rather than like a piggy bank.

Summary

Your business is your most valuable investment, and it is important that you have an investment plan to grow its value. The starting point is setting a targeted annual growth rate for your business investment. Once your target is set, look at the key factors that impact your business value and determine which of these factors you and your team should focus on to increase the value your business.

It is important that you make this a priority and select the right employees and advisors to assist you on this journey. Don't be afraid to change your goals and strategies as your plan progresses and you obtain more visibility. By setting a course of action, you may not become a millionaire. But you will achieve greater riches than by not putting a plan into place.

Epilogue

Country Club Lifestyle Revisited

I arrived home after a long day of work and could not believe the email that I saw on my computer. It was from the "Country Club Lifestyle" business-woman that I introduced from the first chapter of the book. She wanted me to prepare another valuation. I went to her office and we agreed to proceed with the valuation. I was anxious to see what the value of her company was and if she was going to be able to exit her business at the price she desired.

Did she maintain her country club lifestyle? The answer is "yes," but I am afraid that it is not going to last. *She is still not treating her business like an investment.* The value of her business has decreased from where it was the last time we prepared the valuation, and her exit strategy has changed because her nephew no longer works in the business. It was clear that she was more concerned about maintaining her lifestyle than growing the value of her business. She is now approaching 70 and does not have a specific plan to grow the value of her business or know how she will exit her business. She still wants the big check when she leaves but it appears that she will not exit her business on her terms.

I want to thank you for reading this book, and I hope it has provided you with a better understanding about how a business like yours is valued.

More importantly, I hope that you are now more motivated to grow the value of your business and to start the process of selecting your exit strategy and succession plan. Whether it is gifting your stock to your son or daughter or selling your business for a ridiculous sum of money, it is my desire that you can say with confidence:

Note   You exited your business on your terms!

Appendices

IRS Revenue Ruling 59-60

In valuing the stock of closely held corporations, or the stock of corporations where market quotations are not available, all other available financial data, as well as all relevant factors affecting the fair market value must be considered for estate tax and gift tax purposes. No general formula may be given that is applicable to the many different valuation situations arising in the valuation of such stock. However, the general approach, methods, and factors which must be considered in valuing such securities are outlined.

Revenue Ruling 54-77, C.B. 1954-1, 187, superseded.

Section 1. Purpose

The purpose of this Revenue Ruling is to outline and review in general the approach, methods and factors to be considered in valuing shares of the capital stock of closely held corporations for estate tax and gift tax purposes. The methods discussed herein will apply likewise to the valuation of corporate stocks on which market quotations are either unavailable or are of such scarcity that they do not reflect the fair market value.

Sec. 2. Background and Definitions

.01 All valuations must be made in accordance with the applicable provisions of the Internal Revenue Code of 1954 [*2] and the Federal Estate Tax and Gift Tax Regulations. Sections 2031(a), 2032 and 2512(a) of the 1954 Code (sections 811 and 1005 of the 1939 Code) require that the property to be included in the gross estate, or made the subject of a gift, shall be taxed on the basis of the value of the property at the time of death of the decedent, the alternate date if so elected, or the date of gift.

.02 Section 20.2031-1(b) of the Estate Tax Regulations (section 81.10 of the Estate Tax Regulations 105) and section 25.2512-1 of the Gift Tax Regulations (section 86.19 of Gift Tax Regulations 108) define fair market value, in effect, as the price at which the property would change hands between a willing buyer and a willing seller when the former is not under any compulsion to buy and the latter is not under any compulsion to sell, both parties having reasonable knowledge of relevant facts. Court decisions frequently state in addition that the hypothetical buyer and seller are assumed to be able, as well as willing, to trade and to be well informed about the property and concerning the market for such property.

.03 Closely held corporations are those corporations the shares of which are owned [*3] by a relatively limited number of stockholders. Often the entire stock issue is held by one family. The result of this situation is that little, if any, trading in the shares takes place. There is, therefore, no established market for the stock and such sales as occur at irregular intervals seldom reflect all of the elements of a representative transaction as defined by the term "fair market value." {238}

Sec. 3. Approach to Valuation

.01 A determination of fair market value, being a question of fact, will depend upon the circumstances in each case. No formula can be devised that will be generally applicable to the multitude of different valuation issues arising in estate and gift tax cases. Often, an appraiser will find wide differences of opinion as to the fair market value of a particular stock. In resolving such differences, he should maintain a reasonable attitude in recognition of the fact that valuation is not an exact science. A sound valuation will be based upon all the relevant facts, but the elements of common sense, informed judgment and reasonableness must enter into the process of weighing those facts and determining their aggregate significance.

.02 [*4] The fair market value of specific shares of stock will vary as general economic conditions change from "normal" to "boom" or "depression," that is, according to the degree of optimism or pessimism with which the investing public regards the future at the required date of appraisal. Uncertainty as to the stability or continuity of the future income from a property decreases its value by increasing the risk of loss of earnings and value in the future. The value of shares of stock of a company with very uncertain future prospects is highly speculative. The appraiser must exercise his judgment as to the degree of risk attaching to the business of the corporation which issued the stock, but that judgment must be related to all of the other factors affecting value.

.03 Valuation of securities is, in essence, a prophesy as to the future and must be based on facts available at the required date of appraisal. As a generalization, the prices of stocks which are traded in volume in a free and active market by informed persons best reflect the consensus of the investing public as to what the future holds for the corporations and industries represented. When a stock is closely held, is traded [*5] infrequently, or is traded in an erratic market, some other measure of value must be used. In many instances, the next best measure may be found in the prices at which the stocks of companies engaged in the same or a similar line of business are selling in a free and open market.

Sec. 4. Factors to Consider

.01 It is advisable to emphasize that in the valuation of the stock of closely held corporations or the stock of corporations where market quotations are either lacking or too scarce to be recognized, all available financial data, as well as all relevant factors affecting the fair market value, should be considered. The following factors, although not all-inclusive are fundamental and require careful analysis in each case:

(a) The nature of the business and the history of the enterprise from its inception.

(b) The economic outlook in general and the condition and outlook of the specific industry in particular.

(c) The book value of the stock and the financial condition of the business.

(d) The earning capacity of the company.

(e) The dividend-paying capacity.

(f) Whether or not the enterprise has goodwill or other intangible value. {239}

(g) Sales of the [*6] stock and the size of the block of stock to be valued.

(h) The market price of stocks of corporations engaged in the same or a similar line of business having their stocks actively traded in a free and open market, either on an exchange or over-the-counter.

.02 The following is a brief discussion of each of the foregoing factors:

(a) The history of a corporate enterprise will show its past stability or instability, its growth or lack of growth, the diversity or lack of diversity of its operations, and other facts needed to form an opinion of the degree of risk involved in the business. For an enterprise which changed its form of organization but carried on the same or closely similar operations of its predecessor, the history of the former enterprise should be considered. The detail to be considered should increase with approach to the required date of appraisal, since recent events are of greatest help in predicting the future; but a study of gross and net income, and of dividends covering a long prior period, is highly desirable. The history to be studied should include, but need not be limited to, the nature of the business, its products or services, its operating and [*7] investment assets, capital structure, plant facilities, sales records and management, all of which should be considered as of the date of the appraisal, with due regard for recent significant changes. Events of the past that are unlikely to recur in the future should be discounted, since value has a close relation to future expectancy.

(b) A sound appraisal of a closely held stock must consider current and prospective economic conditions as of the date of appraisal, both in the national economy and in the industry or industries with which the corporation is allied. It is important to know that the company is more or less successful than its competitors in the same industry, or that it is maintaining a stable position with respect to competitors. Equal or even greater significance may attach to the ability of the industry with which the company is allied to compete with other industries. Prospective competition which has not been a factor in prior years should be given careful attention. For example, high profits due to the novelty of its product and the lack of competition often lead to increasing competition. The public's appraisal of the future prospects of competitive industries [*8] or of competitors within an industry may be indicated by price trends in the markets for commodities and for securities. The loss of the manager of a so-called "one-man" business may have a depressing effect upon the value of the stock of such business, particularly if there is a lack of trained personnel capable of succeeding to the management of the enterprise. In valuing the stock of this type of business, therefore, the effect of the loss of the manager on the future expectancy of the business, and the absence of management-succession potentialities are pertinent factors to be taken into consideration. On the other hand, there may be factors which offset, in whole or in part, the loss of the manager's services. For instance, the nature of the business and of its assets may be such that they will not be impaired by the loss of the manager. Furthermore, the loss may be adequately covered by life insurance, or competent management might be employed on the basis of the consideration paid for the former manager's services. These, or other {240} offsetting factors, if found to exist, should be carefully weighed against the loss of the manager's services in valuing the stock [*9] of the enterprise.

(c) Balance sheets should be obtained, preferably in the form of comparative annual statements for two or more years immediately preceding the date of appraisal, together with a balance sheet at the end of the month preceding that date, if corporate accounting will permit. Any balance sheet descriptions that are not self-explanatory, and balance sheet items comprehending diverse assets or liabilities, should be clarified in essential detail by supporting supplemental schedules. These statements usually will disclose to the appraiser

(1) liquid position (ratio of current assets to current liabilities); (2) gross and net book value of principal classes of fixed assets; (3) working capital; (4) long-term indebtedness; (5) capital structure; and (6) net worth. Consideration also should be given to any assets not essential to the operation of the business, such as investments in securities, real estate, etc. In general, such nonoperating assets will command a lower rate of return than do the operating assets, although in exceptional cases the reverse may be true. In computing the book value per share of stock, assets of the investment type should be revalued on [*10] the basis of their market price and the book value adjusted accordingly. Comparison of the company's balance sheets over several years may reveal, among other facts, such developments as the acquisition of additional production facilities or subsidiary companies, improvement in financial position, and details as to recapitalizations and other changes in the capital structure of the corporation. If the corporation has more than one class of stock outstanding, the charter or certificate of incorporation should be examined to ascertain the explicit rights and privileges of the various stock issues including: (1) voting powers, (2) preference as to dividends, and (3) preference as to assets in the event of liquidation.

(d) Detailed profit-and-loss statements should be obtained and considered for a representative period immediately prior to the required date of appraisal, preferably five or more years. Such statements should show (1) gross income by principal items; (2) principal deductions from gross income including major prior items of operating expenses, interest and other expense on each item of long-term debt, depreciation and depletion if such deductions are made, officers' [*11] salaries, in total if they appear to be reasonable or in detail if they seem to be excessive, contributions (whether or not deductible for tax purposes) that the nature of its business and its community position require the corporation to make, and taxes by principal items, including income and excess profits taxes; (3) net income available for dividends; (4) rates and amounts of dividends paid on each class of stock; (5) remaining amount carried to surplus; and (6) adjustments to, and reconciliation with, surplus as stated on the balance sheet. With profit and loss statements of this character available, the appraiser should be able to separate recurrent from nonrecurrent items of income and expense, to distinguish between operating income and investment income, and to ascertain whether or not any line of business in which the company is engaged is operated consistently at a loss and might be abandoned with benefit to the company. The percentage of earnings retained for business expansion should be {241} noted when dividend-paying capacity is considered. Potential future income is a major factor in many valuations of closely-held stocks, and all information concerning past income [*12] which will be helpful in predicting the future should be secured. Prior earnings records usually are the most reliable guide as to the future expectancy, but resort to arbitrary five-or-ten-year averages without regard to current trends or future prospects will not produce a realistic valuation. If, for instance, a record of progressively increasing or decreasing net income is found, then greater weight may be accorded the most recent years' profits in estimating earning power. It will be helpful, in judging risk and the extent to which a business is a marginal operator, to consider deductions from income and net income in terms of percentage of sales. Major categories of cost and expense to be so analyzed include the consumption of raw materials and supplies in the case of manufacturers, processors and fabricators; the cost of purchased merchandise in the case of merchants; utility services; insurance; taxes; depletion or depreciation; and interest.

(e) Primary consideration should be given to the dividend-paying capacity of the company rather than to dividends actually paid in the past. Recognition must be given to the necessity of retaining a reasonable portion of profits [*13] in a company to meet competition. Dividend-paying capacity is a factor that must be considered in an appraisal, but dividends actually paid in the past may not have any relation to dividend-paying capacity. Specifically, the dividends paid by a closely held family company may be measured by the income needs of the stockholders or by their desire to avoid taxes on dividend receipts, instead of by the ability of the company to pay dividends. Where an actual or effective controlling interest in a corporation is to be valued, the dividend factor is not a material element, since the payment of such dividends is discretionary with the controlling stockholders. The individual or group in control can substitute salaries and bonuses for dividends, thus reducing net income and understating the dividend-paying capacity of the company. It follows, therefore, that dividends are less reliable criteria of fair market value than other applicable factors.

(f) In the final analysis, goodwill is based upon earning capacity. The presence of goodwill and its value, therefore, rests upon the excess of net earnings over and above a fair return on the net tangible assets. While the element of goodwill [*14] may be based primarily on earnings, such factors as the prestige and renown of the business, the ownership of a trade or brand name, and a record of successful operation over a prolonged period in a particular locality, also may furnish support for the inclusion of intangible value. In some instances it may not be possible to make a separate appraisal of the tangible and intangible assets of the business. The enterprise has a value as an entity. Whatever intangible value there is, which is supportable by the facts, may be measured by the amount by which the appraised value of the tangible assets exceeds the net book value of such assets.

(g) Sales of stock of a closely held corporation should be carefully investigated to determine whether they represent transactions at arm's length. Forced or distress sales do not ordinarily reflect fair market value nor do isolated sales in small amounts necessarily control {242} as the measure of value. This is especially true in the valuation of a controlling interest in a corporation. Since, in the case of closely held stocks, no prevailing market prices are available, there is no basis for making an adjustment for blockage. It follows, [*15] therefore, that such stocks should be valued upon a consideration of all the evidence affecting the fair market value. The size of the block of stock itself is a relevant factor to be considered. Although it is true that a minority interest in an unlisted corporation's stock is more difficult to sell than a similar block of listed stock, it is equally true that control of a corporation, either actual or in effect, representing as it does an added element of value, may justify a higher value for a specific block of stock.

(h) Section 2031(b) of the Code states, in effect, that in valuing unlisted securities the value of stock or securities of corporations engaged in the same or a similar line of business which are listed on an exchange should be taken into consideration along with all other factors. An important consideration is that the corporations to be used for comparisons have capital stocks which are actively traded by the public. In accordance with section 2031(b) of the Code, stocks listed on an exchange are to be considered first. However, if sufficient comparable companies whose stocks are listed on an exchange cannot be found, other comparable companies which have [*16] stocks actively traded in on the over-the-counter market also may be used. The essential factor is that whether the stocks are sold on an exchange or over-the-counter there is evidence of an active, free public market for the stock as of the valuation date. In selecting corporations for comparative purposes, care should be taken to use only comparable companies. Although the only restrictive requirement as to comparable corporations specified in the statute is that their lines of business be the same or similar, yet it is obvious that consideration must be given to other relevant factors in order that the most valid comparison possible will be obtained. For illustration, a corporation having one or more issues of preferred stock, bonds or debentures in addition to its common stock should not be considered to be directly comparable to one having only common stock outstanding. In like manner, a company with a declining business and decreasing markets is not comparable to one with a record of current progress and market expansion.

Sec. 5. Weight to be Accorded Various Factors

The valuation of closely held corporate stock entails the consideration of all relevant factors as [*17] stated in section 4. Depending upon the circumstances in each case, certain factors may carry more weight than others because of the nature of the company's business. To illustrate:

(a) Earnings may be the most important criterion of value in some cases whereas asset value will receive primary consideration in others. In general, the appraiser will accord primary consideration to earnings when valuing stocks of companies which sell products or services to the public; conversely, in the investment or holding type of company, the appraiser may accord the greatest weight to the assets underlying the security to be valued. {243}

(b) The value of the stock of a closely held investment or real estate holding company, whether or not family owned, is closely related to the value of the assets underlying the stock. For companies of this type the appraiser should determine the fair market values of the assets of the company. Operating expenses of such a company and the cost of liquidating it, if any, merit consideration when appraising the relative values of the stock and the underlying assets. The market values of the underlying assets give due weight to potential earnings and dividends [*18] of the particular items of property underlying the stock, capitalized at rates deemed proper by the investing public at the date of appraisal. A current appraisal by the investing public should be superior to the retrospective opinion of an individual. For these reasons, adjusted net worth should be accorded greater weight in valuing the stock of a closely held investment or real estate holding company, whether or not family owned, than any of the other customary yardsticks of appraisal, such as earnings and dividend paying capacity.

Sec. 6. Capitalization Rates

In the application of certain fundamental valuation factors, such as earnings and dividends, it is necessary to capitalize the average or current results at some appropriate rate. A determination of the proper capitalization rate presents one of the most difficult problems in valuation. That there is no ready or simple solution will become apparent by a cursory check of the rates of return and dividend yields in terms of the selling prices of corporate shares listed on the major exchanges of the country. Wide variations will be found even for companies in the same industry. Moreover, the ratio will fluctuate from [*19] year to year depending upon economic conditions. Thus, no standard tables of capitalization rates applicable to closely held corporations can be formulated. Among the more important factors to be taken into consideration in deciding upon a capitalization rate in a particular case are: (1) the nature of the business; (2) the risk involved; and (3) the stability or irregularity of earnings.

Sec. 7. Average of Factors

Because valuations cannot be made on the basis of a prescribed formula, there is no means whereby the various applicable factors in a particular case can be assigned mathematical weights in deriving the fair market value. For this reason, no useful purpose is served by taking an average of several factors (for example, book value, capitalized earnings and capitalized dividends) and basing the valuation on the result. Such a process excludes active consideration of other pertinent factors, and the end result cannot be supported by a realistic application of the significant facts in the case except by mere chance.

Sec. 8. Restrictive Agreements

Frequently, in the valuation of closely held stock for estate and gift tax purposes, it will be found that the stock [*20] is subject to an agreement restricting its sale or transfer. Where shares of stock were acquired by a decedent subject to an option reserved by the issuing corporation to repurchase at a certain price, the option price is usually accepted as the fair market value for estate tax purposes. See Rev. Rul. 54-76, C.B. 1954-1, 194. However, in such case the option price is not {244} determinative of fair market value for gift tax purposes. Where the option, or buy and sell agreement, is the result of voluntary action by the stockholders and is binding during the life as well as at the death of the stockholders, such agreement may or may not, depending upon the circumstances of each case, fix the value for estate tax purposes. However, such agreement is a factor to be considered, with other relevant factors, in determining fair market value. Where the stockholder is free to dispose of his shares during life and the option is to become effective only upon his death, the fair market value is not limited to the option price. It is always necessary to consider the relationship of the parties, the relative number of shares held by the decedent, and other material facts, to determine [*21] whether the agreement represents a bonafide business arrangement or is a device to pass the decedent's shares to the natural objects of his bounty for less than an adequate and full consideration in money or money's worth. In this connection see Rev. Rul. 157 C.B. 1953-2, 255, and Rev. Rul. 189, C.B. 1953-2, 294.

Sample Engagement Letter

January 30, 2013

Charlie Sample

Chairman & CEO

Fantastic Footballs, Inc.

Sample, Ohio 99999

Dear Mr. Sample:

We appreciate the opportunity to provide you our valuation services. This letter outlines our understanding of the terms and objectives of the engagement.

We will perform a valuation of your common stock interest in Fantastic Footballs, Inc. for business planning purposes. Our valuation will include a per share value on both a controlling and noncontrolling interest. The date of the valuation will be as of December 31, 2012.

We will provide you with two opinions of value. The standards of value that will be used in this engagement are "fair market value" and "investment value." The term "fair market value" is defined as follows:

> *The price at which the property would change hands between a willing buyer and a willing seller, neither being under a compulsion to buy or sell and both having reasonable knowledge of relevant facts.* ·

The term "investment value" is defined as follows:

> *The price to a specific buyer or investor often based on perceived synergies when the business is combined with another business.*

We plan to start the engagement when your staff is available to provide us with the requested information, and unless unforeseen problems are encountered, we will provide you with a report draft within 45 days of receiving all requested documents.

In performing our valuation, we will be relying upon the accuracy and reliability of the operations' historical financial statements, forecasts of future operations, or other financial data. We will not audit, compile, or review those financial statements, forecasts, or financial data and will not express an opinion or any form of assurance on them. Our engagement cannot be relied upon to disclose errors, irregularities, or illegal acts, including fraud or defalcations, that may exist. At the conclusion of the engagement, we will ask you or any authorized official of the Company to sign a representation letter on the accuracy and reliability of the financial information used in the engagement.

We will document the results of the engagement in a full valuation report. We understand our valuation conclusion will serve as a basis for the stated purpose in this letter, and the distribution of the report is restricted to this purpose and will not be used for any other purpose or by any unintended user, or with respect to any other date. We have no responsibility to update our valuation report for events and circumstances that occur after the date of its issuance. If for any reason we are unable to complete the valuation engagement, we will not issue a report as a result of the engagement.

Our method of valuation follows the guidelines set forth by the Internal Revenue Service (IRS) in its Revenue Ruling 59-60, as well as conforming to the appraisal standards promulgated by the American Society of Appraisers and the AICPA.

The fee for our valuation service and the final report will be $ XXXX. We will send you progress invoices on a monthly basis. All invoices will be due and payable upon receipt. A service charge of X% per annum will be added to past due balances. If fees become more than 90 days past due, we will discontinue work on your account until the balance is paid in full. No other services will be provided to you after the delivery of the final report unless there is a written agreement addressing the cost for and the work to be performed.

We appreciate this opportunity to be of service to you and look forward to working with you on this important engagement. If you agree with the forego-ing terms, please sign the copy of this letter in the space provided below and return a signed copy back to us.

Sincerely,

Tim McDaniel, CPA/ABV, ASA, CBA

Director of Valuation & Succession Planning Services

_____

Signature

_____

Date

Sample Due Diligence Request

The following is a list of documents and other information that a buyer may request during the due diligence process. Each buyer and transaction is unique, and what is requested will differ among buyers. This sample is only intended to provide you with a general idea of items that may be requested from you in an M&A transaction and should not be considered as a complete list.

Organization and Records

- A staff organization chart, listing all employees with titles and grade levels and any open positions.

- Biographies and resumes for all company executives.

- Employee Handbook (including new employee orientation documents). Provide the human resources policies relating to sexual harassment, background investigations, and drug testing.

- Copy of articles or certificate of incorporation and any amendments.

- Copy of by-laws or code of regulations and any amendments.
- Copy of all resolutions and minutes of board of director meetings.
- List of states where the company conducts business and a list of states where the company has obtained a Certificate of Good Standing.
- List of stockholders and their stock ownership (include stock options or similar rights, if applicable).
- All stockholders' agreements and other agreements relating to transfer restrictions or voting rights with respect to any equity securities.
- Any agreements relating to partnerships or a joint venture that the company is part of.
- Copies of the company's documentation retention or destruction policy.

Financial Statements and Records

General

- Annual financial statements from an outside accountant for the past five years.
- Internal financial statements for the most recent year to date and a comparison statement for the similar period of the prior year.
- Auditor's review letters and management letters for the last five years.
- Operating budgets and capital expenditure budgets for the most recent year, the current year, and any future periods.
- Description of any changes in accounting methods during the past five years.

Assets

- List of all bank accounts (including name of bank, owner of the account, the account number, current balance, and authorized signatories).
- Accounts receivable aging report as of the most recent month end.

- List of accounts in dispute or collection proceedings.

- Total of credit balances owed to customers as of latest month end.

- Fixed-asset detail listing with depreciation schedules as of the latest fiscal year.

- List of actual capital expenditures for past three years and year to date.

- List of all real property used by the business by location, including street address, county, and state. Indicate whether such real property is owned or leased.

- Inventory aging report as of the most recent month end. Identify all inventories that are greater than 180 days.

- UCC searches for all assets, together with a description of all liens or security interests.

- Schedule and copies of all leases (both capital and operating) and installment purchase contracts with annual minimum commitments in excess of $10,000.

- All material deeds, leases (for real estate or personal property), or options to purchase personal property.

- All reports, surveys, studies (including environmental reports), and independent appraisals of all land or other property that is either owned or leased by the company.

Liabilities

- Schedule of all outstanding long-term and short-term debt (other than normal trade payables) including payee, origination date, due date, interest rate, monthly payment, security and current balance.

- All loan agreements and credit instruments, debt instruments, indentures, security agreements, mortgages, promissory notes, guarantees and letters of credit, and other similar instruments evidencing borrowings and any related security documents.

- All other material agreements with creditors, including any documentation with respect to representations given to creditors in connection with obtaining credit.

- List of all mortgages, liens, and security interests in properties belonging to the company.

- All agreements or other documents relating to any loans or advances to, or investments in, other entities.

- Computation demonstrating compliance with financial covenants in existing financing documents.

- List of all obligations that are not listed on the balance sheet in excess of $10,000.

Salaries and Benefits

- List of all employees, together with job descriptions, actual compensation for prior year, and targeted compensation for current year.

- Written description of compensation formula (i.e., salary plus incentive compensation plus anything else), related pay dates, and the pay periods covered.

- Year-to-date and prior-year quarterly payroll tax returns (Form 941).

- IRS Form 5500 for prior three years. Include the summary annual reports for qualified pension or 401(k) plans, profit sharing plans, and health & welfare plans.

- Current plan documents and all amendments since inception of plan(s) pertaining to qualified pension/401(k) and profit sharing plans, including summary plan descriptions and a summary of material modifications.

- Current plan documents and all amendments for any deferred-compensation plans.

- Most recent favorable determination letter and copy of IRS Form 5300 and supporting documents.

- Copy of the investment management agreement and plan administration agreement with record keeper, including latest invoice for services.

- Notices from Department of Labor and IRS since inception of plan, including any notices concerning Form 5500 reporting deficiencies related to late filings and plan audit matters.

- Plan investment records for most recent plan year pertaining to qualified pension and profit sharing plans.

- Contribution history for prior three years pertaining to qualified pension and profit sharing plans.

- Copies of discrimination test results for prior three years pertaining to all retirement plans and cafeteria plans.

- Current plan documents, amendments, and summary plan descriptions pertaining to health care plan.

- Copies of insurance contracts and service agreements, including most recent invoices, pertaining to health care plan.

- A summary of the vacation policy.

- A summary of other paid time-off policies (sickness, holidays, and jury duty).

- List of vacation hours accrued but not yet taken for each employee as of the most recent year end.

- Copies of workers' compensation filings and a list of all claims that have occurred during the past five years.

Tax-related Items

- Copies of federal, state, and local tax returns for the past five years.

- Copies of any settlement documents, correspondence from taxing authorities, currently pending tax disputes, proceedings, or issues for the preceding five years.

- Information regarding extension of statutes, if applicable.

- Any private letter rulings or other correspondence about specific tax issues with the IRS.

- Status and list of any audits in progress (federal, state, and local).

- Copies of any special tax elections filed by the company.

- Copies of sales-and-use tax returns for last three years.

- Copies of property tax returns for last three years.

- Description of any tax abatement or incentive agreements.

Employee Matters

- Copies of all contracts or commitments for the employment of any employee, independent contractor, consultant, or advisor.

- Copies of all agreements, contracts, or commitments relating to any bonus, deferred compensation, pension, profit sharing, stock option, employee stock purchase, retirement, medical life insurance, disability, or other employee benefit plan.

- Copies of covenants not to compete and secrecy agreements with any employee or former employee, which are still valid.

- Description of past labor disputes, requests for arbitration, strikes and other labor disruptions, complaints, or other claims of unfair labor practices and material grievance proceedings.

- Copy of the current union agreement and status of current negotiations.

- Description of any material, oral agreements, or understandings with employees.

- Statement of the licensure status of all professional employees.

Market and Sales Overview

- Description of the size of the market and how the market is segmented.

- Any forecast of the market's projected growth.

- Detailed summary of the profitability by product, customer, and segment.

- List of new products in the pipeline and estimates of the remaining time and expense required to launch each new product.

- List of sales to the top ten customers for the past three years and a description of how long the company had sales relationships with the top ten customers.

- Description of the sales process through the Internet.

- Description of any customer contracts that are coming up for renewal and any likely changes to the key terms of those agreements.

- Details of history of complaints from customers and a list of any customers who have indicated that they will no longer be a customer in the future.

- Results of any customer satisfaction surveys.

Material Contracts and Other Documents

- List of all vendors or suppliers.

- List of purchases by vendor for the ten largest vendors for the latest two fiscal years and year to date.

- Web site hosting and connectivity agreements.

- Copies of all contracts and agreements for the future purchase of materials, supplies, equipment, or services that calls for or could result in payments of more than $10,000.

- Copies of all current and future contracts and agreements for the sale of products or services that exceed $10,000.

- Copies of noncompete or similar agreements which restrict or limit the company or its representatives from engaging in any type of business.

- Copies of any contracts, instruments, judgments, or decrees that might reasonably be expected to adversely affect the business practices, operations, or condition of the company or any property.

- Description of any material oral agreements or understandings.

- Copies of all documents and agreements evidencing other material financing arrangements including sale-and-leaseback arrangements and installment purchases.

- Copies of all secrecy, confidentiality, and nondisclosure agreements to which the company is a party.

- Copies of all contracts or agreements to which directors, officers, or shareholders of the company (or members of their families) are parties.

- Copies of all material permits, licenses, or governmental consents required to conduct the business of the company as it is now conducted.

- Copies of all reports filed and significant correspondence with any state or federal regulatory agency during the past three years.

- Description of the company's use of and policies regarding independent contractors and the amount of payment in current and prior year.

Legal and Litigation Matters

- Schedule of all litigation, administrative, regulatory, or judicial proceedings or governmental investigations pending or threatened by or against the company, including the name of the case, nature of the suit, amount sought in the complaint, name and location of the court in which the case is pending, and estimated amount of potential judgment.

- Schedule and summary of all litigation or other proceedings settled or otherwise resolved within the past five years.

- Documentation regarding any litigation or other proceeding involving any officer or director of the company concerning bankruptcy, crimes, securities, or business practices.

- Copies of all consent decrees, judgments, other decrees or orders, settlement agreements, and other agreements to which the company is a party.

- Copies of all notices or demand letters regarding or relating to any material claims by or against the company with respect to which no litigation has yet been filed.

- Copies of all notices, citations, and other communications received in the past three years from any governmental agency filed in regards to the company in its business operations, or compliance with any applicable governmental regulations.

- Copies of insurance company loss runs for all coverages, including auto liability, and general and professional liability coverage for the past five years.

- Copies of any open charges of discrimination, complaints, or related litigation, or any such cases that have been closed within the past five years.

- Schedule of warranty claims.

- Copy of all legal invoices for the past three years.

Intellectual Property

- List of all patents, patent applications, trademarks, service marks, trade names, copyrights, know-how, and trade secrets owned or used by the company with the status of each.

- Itemized list of all potential patents that have not been applied for.

- All unregistered trademarks and service marks used by the organization.

- All copyright registrations.

- Copies of all material license agreements pertaining to software or other intangible assets.

- Product documentation and manuals for the company's software, databases, and networks (or other description of primary capabilities).

- Copies of all licenses of intellectual property in which the company is the licensor or licensee.

- List of the company's Internet sites and newsgroups.

- Copies of any royalty agreements (whether the company pays or receives the royalty).

- Summary of research-and-development expenditures over the last five years.

Miscellaneous

- Description of any earn-outs or contingent consideration related to any completed acquisitions.

- Schedule of all transactions with related parties (or their families) and future obligations.

- List of all outside consultants and the services performed during the past five years. Copies of any reports received from any consultants, including environmental, human resources, and marketing.

- Description of the backup systems in place with offsite storage, both for the corporate-level databases and for individual computers.

- Any other document or information that is significant with respect to the business of the company.

Sample Family Business Creed

Preamble

From many open discussions among us regarding our family values and our aspirations for both our family and our business, most recently crystallized at our family strategic planning session, we have agreed on certain binding principles and practices in the highest and best interests of harmony in our family and the opportunity for a brilliant future in the business for all those involved.

This Creed was developed and agreed to in recognition of our Company's past financial success, devoted employees, its public responsibility, and the challenging fact that less than 10% of successful family businesses make it through the third generation. Our third generation will be an active part of this business, and we want to allow them the same opportunities that have been enjoyed by prior generations and for them to provide opportunities for the fourth generation.

Our Agreement

Management Philosophy and Objectives

Our Company will be managed by a strategic management philosophy that combines the highest individual and business principles. Our highest priority will be the continuation of the business into future generations.

We view our Company as a valued family heritage started by Mr. Sample. We want to continue as a family-owned business that is stable, growing, and profitable, with the understanding that our priorities lie more in honoring our responsibility to each other rather than the profit or economic return individually. Our responsibility to each other includes loyalty, respect, trust, honesty, and working as a cohesive unit. We believe that if we honor these values and run our business properly, the economic return will follow.

We will continue the tradition started by our founder of community involvement through financial gifts and volunteer activities.

We will not compromise sound business principles or our family values for profits or personal economic gain. The security of our employees and our family depends upon the integrity of this commitment, and each of us herewith commits, in good faith, never, for any reason, to place pressure on Company officials or its board of directors for dividends, employment requests, or other benefits beyond what Company management and the board in its sole discretion feel are consistent with the above stated objectives.

Positions in the Company

Family members who have a great enthusiasm for our business will be welcomed to work full time in the Company. Entry into the business will be an opportunity and not a birthright, and family members will be held to higher levels of commitment and performance than nonfamily employees.

Family members who aspire to management roles must have a bachelor's degree or equivalent work experience. It is preferred that the family member obtain some experience outside of the Company prior to entering management. Each family member must complete a formal training program provided by the management team that allows for at least three months of training in each major functional area of the business.

We agree that no one, least of all a family member, should be in this Company unless they have a passionate enthusiasm for their work and demonstrate excellence in their work. This will be evident by their attitude, work product, and time spent on their work. In the event that a family member's performance does not consistently measure up to this criteria, he/she may be requested to leave.

In order to limit the potential for future conflict, we hereby agree that, with all love and respect, no in-laws shall hold positions in the Company.

Leadership

Selection of all management positions will be based on professional competence. It is our hope and desire that at all times a family member will be the chief executive officer of the Company, and we pledge our positive and full support to that person even if we may have preferred another choice. We have established that our next leader should satisfy the following criteria:

- Must have leadership qualities, the ability to command respect among employees and family members, and vision for the Company's future.

- Must have a wide variety of experience and be an appropriate ambassador to our customers, the community, and the business world.

- Must have a proven track record of business performance.

- Must go through a rigorous background check and be interviewed by an outside human resource consultant.

Compensation of Family Members

Family members who work in the business will be compensated on the same basis as their peers in our industry. They will participate in the same performance evaluation process that is accorded employees, including at least one annual written evaluation by their direct supervisor and to be reviewed by the chief executive officer and the board of directors.

Voting Control and Stock Ownership

Only bloodline family members and their direct bloodline descendants may own stock in the Company or vote. Voting control will be vested only in family members who are personally active as employees in the business. No stock in the Company may be sold or transferred by any family member, other than to direct bloodline descendants, without first being offered for sale back to the Company at an independently appraised value. All stock transactions are subject to the most recent buy-sell agreement and closed corporation agreement.

Each family member will discuss that importance of continuity of the business within our family bloodline to their future spouses. No nonbloodline family member will be able to own stock at anytime. It is our desire to discuss this with our future spouses and have them agree to this in writing prior to marriage.

Communication

We will continue to have open and candid communication within the family. This will include at least one annual meeting of our "Family Council," which shall include in-laws and children who are ready to begin an understanding of the Company.

We will respect the opinions of other family members even if we don't agree with them. In the event of disagreements, we commit to constructive resolution that places the best interests of the Company and the family over our own preferences.

Our Employees

The success of our enterprise would not have been possible without our devoted, loyal, and hardworking employees. We are committed to the continuance of an environment that values their contribution, treats them with respect, and provides them with appropriate rewards and benefits. Our reward system should be based on the employee's ability to meet long-term objectives. We will provide our employees with a competitive salary, an attractive benefit package, and incentivize them to stay with the Company long-term.

Amendment of This Creed

We will together review this Family Creed from time to time (at least every three years) and will amend or modify it only by majority vote of family bloodline members in the business that are over the age of 18. Although this is not a legally binding document, unless it is amended, we pledge to support it without reservation and to enforce it among our children to the best of our ability.

We agree that this Creed is adopted, effective as of this date.

_____   _____

_____   _____

_____   _____

AICPA Statement on Standards for Valuation Services No. 1

Excerpts for Valuation Reports and Glossary of Valuation Terms*

The Valuation Report

47. A valuation report is a written or oral communication to the client containing the conclusion of value or the calculated value of the subject interest. Reports issued for purposes of certain controversy proceedings are exempt from this reporting standard (paragraph 50).

48. The three types of written reports that a valuation analyst may use to communicate the results of an engagement to estimate value are: for a valuation engagement, a detailed report or a summary report; and for a calculation engagement, a calculation report.

For a Valuation Engagement

a. *Detailed Report:* This report may be used only to communicate the results of a valuation engagement (conclusion of value); it should not be used to communicate the results of a calculation engagement (calculated value) (paragraph 51).

b. *Summary Report:* This report may be used only to communicate the results of a valuation engagement (conclusion of value); it should not be used to communicate the results of a calculation engagement (calculated value) (paragraph 71).

For a valuation engagement, the determination of whether to prepare a detailed report or a summary report is based on the level of reporting detail agreed to by the valuation analyst and the client.

49. The valuation analyst should indicate in the valuation report the restrictions on the use of the report (which may include restrictions on the users of the report, the uses of the report by such users, or both) (paragraph 65(d)).

Reporting Exemption for Certain Controversy Proceedings

50. A valuation performed for a matter before a court, an arbitrator, a mediator or other facilitator, or a matter in a governmental or administrative proceeding, is exempt from the reporting provisions of this Statement. The reporting exemption applies whether the matter proceeds to trial or settles. The exemption applies only to the reporting provisions of this Statement (paragraphs 47–49 and 51–78). The developmental provisions of the Statement (paragraphs 21–46) still apply whenever the valuation analyst expresses a conclusion of value or a calculated value (Valuation Services Interpretation No. 1).

Detailed Report

51. The detailed report is structured to provide sufficient information to permit intended users to understand the data, reasoning, and analyses underlying the valuation analyst's conclusion of value. A detailed report should include, as applicable, the following sections titled using wording similar in content to that shown:

- Letter of transmittal

- Table of contents

- Introduction

- Sources of information

- Analysis of the subject entity and related nonfinancial information

- Financial statement/information analysis

- Valuation approaches and methods considered

- Valuation approaches and methods used

- Valuation adjustments

- Nonoperating assets, nonoperating liabilities, and excess or deficient operating assets (if any)

- Representation of the valuation analyst

- Reconciliation of estimates and conclusion of value

- Qualifications of the valuation analyst

- Appendices and exhibits

The above listed report sections and the detailed information within the sections described in the following paragraphs 52–77 may be positioned in the body of the report or elsewhere in the report at the discretion of the valuation analyst.

Introduction

52. This section should provide an overall description of the valuation engagement. The information in the section should be sufficient to enable the intended user of the report to understand the nature and scope of the

valuation engagement, as well as the work performed. The introduction section may include, among other things, the following information:

a. Identity of the client

b. Purpose and intended use of the valuation

c. Intended users of the valuation

d. Identity of the subject entity

e. Description of the subject interest

f. Whether the business interest has ownership control characteristics and its degree of marketability

g. Valuation date

h. Report date

i. Type of report issued (namely, a detailed report) (paragraph 51)

j. Applicable premise of value

k. Applicable standard of value

l. Assumptions and limiting conditions (alternatively, these often appear in an appendix) (paragraph 18)

m. Any restrictions or limitations in the scope of work or data available for analysis (paragraph 19)

n. Any hypothetical conditions used in the valuation engagement, including the basis for their use (paragraph 22)

o. If the work of a specialist was used in the valuation engagement, a description of how the specialist's work was relied upon (paragraph 20)

p. Disclosure of subsequent events in certain circumstances (paragraph 43)

q. Any application of the jurisdictional exception (paragraph 10)

r. Any additional information the valuation analyst deems useful to enable the user(s) of the report to understand the work performed

If the above items are not included in the introduction, they should be included elsewhere in the valuation report.

Sources of Information

53. This section of the report should identify the relevant sources of information used in performing the valuation engagement. It may include, among other things, the following:

   a. For valuation of a business, business ownership interest, or security, whether and to what extent the subject entity's facilities were visited

   b. For valuation of an intangible asset, whether the legal registration, contractual documentation, or other tangible evidence of the asset was inspected

   c. Names, positions, and titles of persons interviewed and their relationships to the subject interest

   d. Financial information (paragraphs 54 and 56)

   e. Tax information (paragraph 55)

   f. Industry data

   g. Market data

   h. Economic data

   i. Other empirical information

   j. Relevant documents and other sources of information provided by or related to the entity

54. If the financial information includes financial statements that were reported on (audit, review, compilation, or attest engagement performed under the Statements on Standards for Attestation Engagements [SSAEs]) by the valuation analyst's firm, the valuation report should disclose this fact and the type of report issued. If the valuation analyst or the valuation analyst's firm did not audit, review, compile, or attest under the SSAEs to the financial information, the valuation analyst should so state and should also state that the valuation analyst assumes no responsibility for the financial information.

55. The financial information may be derived from or may include information derived from tax returns. With regard to such derived information and other tax information (paragraph 53(e)), the valuation analyst should identify the tax returns used and any existing relationship between the valuation analyst and the tax preparer. If the valuation analyst or the valuation analyst's firm did not audit, review, compile, or attest under the SSAEs to any financial information derived from tax returns that is used during the

valuation engagement, the valuation analyst should so state and should also state that the valuation analyst assumes no responsibility for that derived information.

56. If the financial information used was derived from financial statements prepared by management that were not the subject of an audit, review, compilation, or attest engagement performed under the SSAEs, the valuation report should:

- Identify the financial statements
- State that, as part of the valuation engagement, the valuation analyst did not audit, review, compile, or attest under the SSAEs to the financial information and assumes no responsibility for that information

Analysis of the Subject Entity and Related Nonfinancial Information

57. The valuation analyst should include a description of the relevant nonfinancial information listed and discussed in paragraph 27.

Financial Statement / Information Analysis

58. This section should include a description of the relevant information listed in paragraph 29. Such description may include:

a. The rationale underlying any normalization or *control adjustments* to financial information

b. Comparison of current performance with historical performance

c. Comparison of performance with industry trends and norms, where available

Valuation Approaches and Methods Considered

59. This section should state that the valuation analyst has considered the valuation approaches discussed in paragraph 31.

Valuation Approaches and Methods Used

60. In this section, the valuation analyst should identify the valuation methods used under each valuation approach and the rationale for their use.

61. This section should also identify the following for each of the three approaches (if used):

a. Income approach:

- Composition of the representative benefit stream

- Method(s) used, and a summary of the most relevant risk factors considered in selecting the appropriate *discount rate*, the capitalization rate, or both

- Other factors as discussed in paragraph 33

b. Asset-based approach or cost approach:

- *Asset-based approach*: Any adjustments made by the valuation analyst to the relevant balance sheet data

- *Cost approach*: The type of cost used, how this cost was estimated, and, if applicable, the forms of and costs associated with depreciation and obsolescence used under the approach and how those costs were estimated

c. Market approach:

- For the guideline public company method:

    - The selected guideline companies and the process used in their selection

    - The pricing multiples used, how they were used, and the rationale for their selection. If the pricing multiples were adjusted, the rationale for such adjustments

- For the guideline company transactions method, the sales transactions and pricing multiples used, how they were used, and the rationale for their selection. If the pricing multiples were adjusted, the rationale for such adjustments

- For the guideline sales of interests in the subject entity method, the sales transactions used, how they were used, and the rationale for determining that these sales are representative of arm's length transactions

62. When a rule of thumb is used in combination with other methods, the valuation report should disclose the source(s) of data used and how the rule of thumb was applied (paragraph 39).

Valuation Adjustments

63. This section should (a) identify each valuation adjustment considered and determined to be applicable, for example, discount for lack of marketability, (b) describe the rationale for using the adjustment and the factors considered in selecting the amount or percentage used, and (c) describe the pre-adjustment value to which the adjustment was applied (paragraph 40).

Nonoperating Assets and Excess Operating Assets

64. When the subject interest is a business, business ownership interest, or security, the valuation report should identify any related nonoperating assets, nonoperating liabilities, or excess or deficient operating assets and their effect on the valuation (paragraph 41).

Representation of the Valuation Analyst

65. Each written report should contain the representation of the valuation analyst. The representation is the section of the report wherein the valuation analyst summarizes the factors that guided his or her work during the engagement. Examples of these factors include the following:

    a. The analyses, opinions, and conclusion of value included in the valuation report are subject to the specified assumptions and limiting conditions (see paragraph 18), and they are the personal analyses, opinions, and conclusion of value of the valuation analyst.

    b. The economic and industry data included in the valuation report have been obtained from various printed or electronic reference sources that the valuation analyst believes to be reliable (any exceptions should be noted). The valuation analyst has not performed any corroborating procedures to substantiate that data.

    c. The valuation engagement was performed in accordance with the American Institute of Certified Public Accountants Statement on Standards for Valuation Services.

d. The parties for which the information and use of the valuation report is restricted are identified; the valuation report is not intended to be and should not be used by anyone other than such parties (paragraph 49).

e. The analyst's compensation is fee-based or is contingent on the outcome of the valuation.

f. The valuation analyst used the work of one or more outside specialists to assist during the valuation engagement. (An outside specialist is a specialist other than those employed in the valuation analyst's firm.) If the work of such a specialist was used, the specialist should be identified. The valuation report should include a statement identifying the level of responsibility, if any, the valuation analyst is assuming for the specialist's work.

g. The valuation analyst has no obligation to update the report or the opinion of value for information that comes to his or her attention after the date of the report.

h. The valuation analyst and the person(s) assuming responsibility for the valuation should sign the representation in their own name(s). The names of those providing significant professional assistance should be identified.

Representations Regarding Information Provided to the Valuation Analyst

66. It may be appropriate for the valuation analyst to obtain written representations regarding information that the subject entity's management provides to the valuation analyst for purposes of his or her performing the valuation engagement. The decision whether to obtain a representation letter is a matter of judgment for the valuation analyst.

Qualifications of the Valuation Analyst

67. The report should contain information regarding the qualifications of the valuation analyst.

Conclusion of Value

68. This section should present a reconciliation of the valuation analyst's estimate or various estimates of the value of the subject interest. In addition to a discussion of the rationale underlying the conclusion of value, this section should include the following or similar statements:

a. A valuation engagement was performed, including the subject interest and the valuation date.

b. The analysis was performed solely for the purpose described in this report, and the resulting estimate of value should not be used for any other purpose.

c. The valuation engagement was conducted in accordance with the Statement(s) on Standards for Valuation Services of the American Institute of Certified Public Accountants.

d. A statement that the estimate of value resulting from a valuation engagement is expressed as a conclusion of value.

e. The scope of work or data available for analysis is explained, including any restrictions or limitations (paragraph 19).

f. A statement describing the conclusion of value, either a single amount or a range.

g. The conclusion of value is subject to the assumptions and limiting conditions (paragraph 18) and to the valuation analyst's representation (paragraph 65).

h. The report is signed in the name of the valuation analyst or the valuation analyst's firm.

i. The date of the valuation report is included.

j. The valuation analyst has no obligation to update the report or the conclusion of value for information that comes to his or her attention after the date of the report.

69. The following is an example of report language that could be used, but is not required, when reporting the results of a valuation engagement:

> We have performed a valuation engagement, as that term is defined in the Statement on Standards for Valuation Services (SSVS) of the American Institute of Certified Public Accountants, of [DEF Company, GHI business ownership interest of DEF Company, GHI security of DEF Company, or GHI intangible asset of DEF Company] as of [valuation date]. This valuation was performed solely to assist in the matter of [purpose of the valuation]; the resulting estimate of value should not be used for any other purpose or by any other party for any purpose. This valuation engagement was conducted in accordance with the SSVS. The estimate of value that results from a valuation engagement is expressed as a conclusion of value.

> [If applicable] We were restricted or limited in the scope of our work or data available for analysis as follows: [describe restrictions or limitations].

> Based on our analysis, as described in this valuation report, the estimate of value of [DEF Company, GHI business ownership interest of DEF Company, GHI security of DEF Company, or GHI intangible asset of DEF Company] as of [valuation date] was [value, either a single amount or a range]. This conclusion is subject to the Statement of Assumptions and Limiting Conditions found in [reference to applicable section of valuation report] and to the Valuation Analyst's Representation found in [reference to applicable section of valuation report]. We have no obligation to update this report or our conclusion of value for information that comes to our attention after the date of this report.

> [Signature]

> [Date]

Appendices and Exhibits

70. Appendices or exhibits may be used for required information or information that supplements the detailed report. Often, the assumptions and limiting conditions and the valuation analyst's representation are provided in appendices to the detailed report.

Summary Report

71. A summary report is structured to provide an abridged version of the information that would be provided in a detailed report, and therefore, need not contain the same level of detail as a detailed report. However, a summary report should, at a minimum, include the following:

    a.   Identity of the client

    b.   Purpose and intended use of the valuation

    c.   Intended users of the valuation

    d.   Identity of the subject entity

    e.   Description of the subject interest

    f.   The business interest's ownership control characteristics, if any, and its degree of marketability

    g.   Valuation date

    h.   Valuation report date

    i.   Type of report issued (namely, a summary report) (paragraph 48)

    j.   Applicable premise of value

    k.   Applicable standard of value

    l.   Sources of information used in the valuation engagement

    m.   Assumptions and limiting conditions of the valuation engagement (paragraph 18)

    n.   The scope of work or data available for analysis including any restrictions or limitations (paragraph 19)

    o.   Any hypothetical conditions used in the valuation engagement, including the basis for their use (paragraph 22)

    p.   If the work of a specialist was used in the valuation (paragraph 20), a description of how the specialist's work was used, and the level of responsibility, if any, the valuation analyst is assuming for the specialist's work

    q.   The valuation approaches and methods used

    r.   Disclosure of subsequent events in certain circumstances (paragraph 43)

s. Any application of the jurisdictional exception (paragraph 10)

t. Representation of the valuation analyst (paragraph 65)

u. The report is signed in the name of the valuation analyst or the valuation analyst's firm

v. A section summarizing the reconciliation of the estimates and the conclusion of value as discussed in paragraphs 68 and 69

APPENDIX A: Ilustrative List of Assumptions and Limiting Conditions for a Business Valuation

The valuation report or calculation report should include a list of assumptions and limiting conditions under which the engagement was performed. This appendix includes an illustrative list of assumptions and limiting conditions that may apply to a business valuation.

Illustrative List of Assumptions and Limiting Conditions

1. The conclusion of value arrived at herein is valid only for the stated purpose as of the date of the valuation.

2. Financial statements and other related information provided by [ABC Company] or its representatives, in the course of this engagement, have been accepted without any verification as fully and correctly reflecting the enterprise's business conditions and operating results for the respective periods, except as specifically noted herein. [Valuation Firm] has not audited, reviewed, or compiled the financial information provided to us and, accordingly, we express no audit opinion or any other form of assurance on this information.

3. Public information and industry and statistical information have been obtained from sources we believe to be reliable. However, we make no representation as to the accuracy or completeness of such information and have performed no procedures to corroborate the information.

4. We do not provide assurance on the achievability of the results forecasted by [ABC Company] because events and circumstances frequently do not occur as expected; differences between actual and expected results may be material; and achievement of the forecasted results is dependent on actions, plans, and assumptions of management.

5. The conclusion of value arrived at herein is based on the assumption that the current level of management expertise and effectiveness would continue to be maintained, and that the character and integrity of the enterprise through any sale, reorganization, exchange, or diminution of the owners' participation would not be materially or significantly changed.

6. This report and the conclusion of value arrived at herein are for the exclusive use of our client for the sole and specific purposes as noted herein. They may not be used for any other purpose or by any other party for any purpose. Furthermore the report and conclusion of value are not intended by the author and should not be construed by the reader to be investment advice in any manner whatsoever. The conclusion of value represents the considered opinion of [Valuation Firm], based on information furnished to them by [ABC Company] and other sources.

7. Neither all nor any part of the contents of this report (especially the conclusion of value, the identity of any valuation specialist(s), or the firm with which such valuation specialists are connected or any reference to any of their professional designations) should be disseminated to the public through advertising media, public relations, news media, sales media, mail, direct transmittal, or any other means of communication without the prior written consent and approval of [Valuation Firm].

8. Future services regarding the subject matter of this report, including, but not limited to testimony or attendance in court, shall not be required of [Valuation Firm] unless previous arrangements have been made in writing.

9. [Valuation Firm] is not an environmental consultant or auditor, and it takes no responsibility for any actual or potential environmental liabilities. Any person entitled to rely on this report, wishing to know whether such liabilities exist, or the scope and their effect on the value of the property, is encouraged to obtain a professional environmental assessment. [Valuation Firm] does not conduct or provide environmental assessments and has not performed one for the subject property.

10. [Valuation Firm] has not determined independently whether [ABC Company] is subject to any present or future liability relating to environmental matters (including, but not limited to CERCLA/Superfund liability) nor the scope of any such liabilities. [Valuation Firm]'s valuation takes no such liabilities into account, except as they have been reported to [Valuation Firm] by [ABC Company] or by an environmental consultant working for [ABC Company], and then only to the extent that the liability was reported to us in an actual or estimated dollar amount. Such matters, if any, are noted in the report. To the extent such information has been reported to us, [Valuation Firm] has relied on it without verification and offers no warranty or representation as to its accuracy or completeness.

11. [Valuation Firm] has not made a specific compliance survey or analysis of the subject property to determine whether it is subject to, or in compliance with, the American Disabilities Act of 1990, and this valuation does not consider the effect, if any, of noncompliance.

12. [Sample wording for use if the jurisdictional exception is invoked.] The conclusion of value (or the calculated value) in this report deviates from the Statement on Standards for Valuation Services as a result of published governmental, judicial, or accounting authority.

13. No change of any item in this appraisal report shall be made by anyone other than [Valuation Firm], and we shall have no responsibility for any such unauthorized change.

14. Unless otherwise stated, no effort has been made to determine the possible effect, if any, on the subject business due to future Federal, state, or local legislation, including any environmental or ecological matters or interpretations thereof.

15. If prospective financial information approved by management has been used in our work, we have not examined or compiled the prospective financial information and therefore, do not express an audit opinion or any other form of assurance on the prospective financial information or the related assumptions. Events and circumstances frequently do not occur as expected and there will usually be differences between prospective financial information and actual results, and those differences may be material.

16. We have conducted interviews with the current management of [ABC Company] concerning the past, present, and prospective operating results of the company.

17. Except as noted, we have relied on the representations of the owners, management, and other third parties concerning the value and useful condition of all equipment, real estate, investments used in the business, and any other assets or liabilities, except as specifically stated to the contrary in this report. We have not attempted to confirm whether or not all assets of the business are free and clear of liens and encumbrances or that the entity has good title to all assets.

APPENDIX B: International Glossary of Business Valuation Terms[†]

To enhance and sustain the quality of business valuations for the benefit of the profession and its clientele, the below identified societies and organizations have adopted the definitions for the terms included in this glossary.

The performance of business valuation services requires a high degree of skill and imposes upon the valuation professional a duty to communicate the valuation process and conclusion in a manner that is clear and not misleading. This duty is advanced through the use of terms whose meanings are clearly established and consistently applied throughout the profession.

If, in the opinion of the business valuation professional, one or more of these terms needs to be used in a manner which materially departs from the enclosed definitions, it is recommended that the term be defined as used within that valuation engagement.

This glossary has been developed to provide guidance to business valuation practitioners by further memorializing the body of knowledge that constitutes the competent and careful determination of value and, more particularly, the communication of how that value was determined.

Departure from this glossary is not intended to provide a basis for civil liability and should not be presumed to create evidence that any duty has been breached.

American Institute of Certified Public Accountants

American Society of Appraisers

Canadian Institute of Chartered Business Valuators

National Association of Certified Valuation Analysts

The Institute of Business Appraisers

Adjusted Book Value Method—a method within the asset approach whereby all assets and liabilities (including off-balance sheet, intangible, and contingent) are adjusted to their fair market values. {NOTE: In Canada on a going concern basis}

[†]Reproduced verbatim from the International Glossary of Business Valuation Terms (the Glossary), which appears at http://bvfls.aicpa.org/Resources/Business+Valuation/Tools+and+ Aids/Definitions+and+Terms/International+Glossary+of+Business+ Valuation+Terms.htm. Note that the phrase, "we discourage the use of this term," that appears herein is also reproduced verbatim.

Arbitrage Pricing Theory—a multivariate model for estimating the cost of equity capital, which incorporates several systematic risk factors.

Asset (Asset-Based) Approach—a general way of determining a value indication of a business, business ownership interest, or security using one or more methods based on the value of the assets net of liabilities.

Beta—a measure of systematic risk of a stock; the tendency of a stock's price to correlate with changes in a specific index.

Blockage Discount—an amount or percentage deducted from the current market price of a publicly traded stock to reflect the decrease in the per share value of a block of stock that is of a size that could not be sold in a reasonable period of time given normal trading volume.

Book Value—see **Net Book Value**.

Business—see **Business Enterprise**.

Business Enterprise—a commercial, industrial, service, or investment entity (or a combination thereof) pursuing an economic activity.

Business Risk—the degree of uncertainty of realizing expected future returns of the business resulting from factors other than financial leverage. See **Financial Risk**.

Business Valuation—the act or process of determining the value of a business enterprise or ownership interest therein.

Capital Asset Pricing Model (CAPM)—a model in which the cost of capital for any stock or portfolio of stocks equals a risk-free rate plus a risk premium that is proportionate to the systematic risk of the stock or portfolio.

Capitalization—a conversion of a single period of economic benefits into value.

Capitalization Factor—any multiple or divisor used to convert anticipated economic benefits of a single period into value.

Capitalization of Earnings Method—a method within the income approach whereby economic benefits for a representative single period are converted to value through division by a capitalization rate.

Capitalization Rate—any divisor (usually expressed as a percentage) used to convert anticipated economic benefits of a single period into value.

Capital Structure—the composition of the invested capital of a business enterprise; the mix of debt and equity financing.

Cash Flow—cash that is generated over a period of time by an asset, group of assets, or business enterprise. It may be used in a general sense to encompass various levels of specifically defined cash flows. When the term is used, it should be supplemented by a qualifier (for example, "discretionary" or "operating") and a specific definition in the given valuation context.

Common Size Statements—financial statements in which each line is expressed as a percentage of the total. On the balance sheet, each line item is shown as a percentage of total assets, and on the income statement, each item is expressed as a percentage of sales.

Control—the power to direct the management and policies of a business enterprise.

Control Premium—an amount or a percentage by which the pro rata value of a controlling interest exceeds the pro rata value of a noncontrolling interest in a business enterprise to reflect the power of control.

Cost Approach—a general way of determining a value indication of an individual asset by quantifying the amount of money required to replace the future service capability of that asset.

Cost of Capital—the expected rate of return that the market requires in order to attract funds to a particular investment.

Debt-Free—*we discourage the use of this term.* See **Invested Capital**.

Discount for Lack of Control—an amount or percentage deducted from the pro rata share of value of 100% of an equity interest in a business to reflect the absence of some or all of the powers of control.

Discount for Lack of Marketability—an amount or percentage deducted from the value of an ownership interest to reflect the relative absence of marketability.

Discount for Lack of Voting Rights—an amount or percentage deducted from the per share value of a minority interest voting share to reflect the absence of voting rights.

Discount Rate—a rate of return used to convert a future monetary sum into present value.

Discounted Cash Flow Method—a method within the income approach whereby the present value of future expected net cash flows is calculated using a discount rate.

Discounted Future Earnings Method—a method within the income approach whereby the present value of future expected economic benefits is calculated using a discount rate.

Economic Benefits—inflows such as revenues, net income, net cash flows, etc.

Economic Life—the period of time over which property may generate economic benefits.

Effective Date—see **Valuation Date**.

Enterprise—see **Business Enterprise**.

Equity—the owner's interest in property after deduction of all liabilities.

Equity Net Cash Flows—those cash flows available to pay out to equity holders (in the form of dividends) after funding operations of the business enterprise, making necessary capital investments, and increasing or decreasing debt financing.

Equity Risk Premium—a rate of return added to a risk-free rate to reflect the additional risk of equity instruments over risk free instruments (a component of the cost of equity capital or equity discount rate).

Excess Earnings—that amount of anticipated economic benefits that exceeds an appropriate rate of return on the value of a selected asset base (often net tangible assets) used to generate those anticipated economic benefits.

Excess Earnings Method—a specific way of determining a value indication of a business, business ownership interest, or security determined as the sum of a) the value of the assets derived by capitalizing excess earnings and b) the value of the selected asset base. Also frequently used to value intangible assets. See **Excess Earnings**.

Fair Market Value—the price, expressed in terms of cash equivalents, at which property would change hands between a hypothetical willing and able buyer and a hypothetical willing and able seller, acting at arm's length in an open and unrestricted market, when neither is under compulsion to buy or sell and when both have reasonable knowledge of the relevant facts. {NOTE: In Canada, the term "price" should be replaced with the term "highest price".}

Fairness Opinion—an opinion as to whether or not the consideration in a transaction is fair from a financial point of view.

Financial Risk—the degree of uncertainty of realizing expected future returns of the business resulting from financial leverage. See **Business Risk**.

Forced Liquidation Value—liquidation value, at which the asset or assets are sold as quickly as possible, such as at an auction.

Free Cash Flow—we discourage the use of this term. See **Net Cash Flow**.

Going Concern—an ongoing operating business enterprise.

Going Concern Value—the value of a business enterprise that is expected to continue to operate into the future. The intangible elements of Going Concern Value result from factors such as having a trained work force, an operational plant, and the necessary licenses, systems, and procedures in place.

Goodwill—that intangible asset arising as a result of name, reputation, customer loyalty, location, products, and similar factors not separately identified.

Goodwill Value—the value attributable to goodwill.

Guideline Public Company Method—a method within the market approach whereby market multiples are derived from market prices of stocks of companies that are engaged in the same or similar lines of business and that are actively traded on a free and open market.

Income (Income-Based) Approach—a general way of determining a value indication of a business, business ownership interest, security, or intangible asset using one or more methods that convert anticipated economic benefits into a present single amount.

Intangible Assets—nonphysical assets such as franchises, trade-marks, patents, copyrights, goodwill, equities, mineral rights, securities, and contracts (as distinguished from physical assets) that grant rights and privileges and have value for the owner.

Internal Rate of Return—a discount rate at which the present value of the future cash flows of the investment equals the cost of the investment.

Intrinsic Value—the value that an investor considers, on the basis of an evaluation or available facts, to be the "true" or "real" value that will become the market value when other investors reach the same conclusion. When the term applies to options, it is the difference between the exercise price and strike price of an option and the market value of the underlying security.

Invested Capital—the sum of equity and debt in a business enterprise. Debt is typically (a) all interest-bearing debt or (b) long-term, interest-bearing debt. When the term is used, it should be supplemented by a specific definition in the given valuation context.

Invested Capital Net Cash Flows—those cash flows available to pay out to equity holders (in the form of dividends) and debt investors (in the form of principal and interest) after funding operations of the business enterprise and making necessary capital investments.

Investment Risk—the degree of uncertainty as to the realization of expected returns.

Investment Value—the value to a particular investor based on individual investment requirements and expectations. {NOTE: In Canada, the term used is "Value to the Owner".}

Key Person Discount—an amount or percentage deducted from the value of an ownership interest to reflect the reduction in value resulting from the actual or potential loss of a key person in a business enterprise.

Levered Beta—the beta reflecting a capital structure that includes debt.

Limited Appraisal—the act or process of determining the value of a business, business ownership interest, security, or intangible asset with limitations in analyses, procedures, or scope.

Liquidity—the ability to quickly convert property to cash or pay a liability.

Liquidation Value—the net amount that would be realized if the business is terminated and the assets are sold piecemeal. Liquidation can be either "orderly" or "forced."

Majority Control—the degree of control provided by a majority position.

Majority Interest—an ownership interest greater than 50% of the voting interest in a business enterprise.

Market (Market-Based) Approach—a general way of determining a value indication of a business, business ownership interest, security, or intangible asset by using one or more methods that compare the subject to similar businesses, business ownership interests, securities, or intangible assets that have been sold.

Market Capitalization of Equity—the share price of a publicly traded stock multiplied by the number of shares outstanding.

Market Capitalization of Invested Capital—the market capitalization of equity plus the market value of the debt component of invested capital.

Market Multiple—the market value of a company's stock or invested capital divided by a company measure (such as economic benefits, number of customers).

Marketability—the ability to quickly convert property to cash at minimal cost.

Marketability Discount—see **Discount for Lack of Marketability**.

Merger and Acquisition Method—a method within the market approach whereby pricing multiples are derived from transactions of significant interests in companies engaged in the same or similar lines of business.

Mid-Year Discounting—a convention used in the Discounted Future Earnings Method that reflects economic benefits being generated at mid-year, approximating the effect of economic benefits being generated evenly throughout the year.

Minority Discount—a discount for lack of control applicable to a minority interest.

Minority Interest—an ownership interest less than 50% of the voting interest in a business enterprise.

Multiple—the inverse of the capitalization rate.

Net Book Value—with respect to a business enterprise, the difference between total assets (net of accumulated depreciation, depletion, and amortization) and total liabilities as they appear on the balance sheet (synonymous with Shareholder's Equity). With respect to a specific asset, the capitalized cost less accumulated amortization or depreciation as it appears on the books of account of the business enterprise.

Net Cash Flows—when the term is used, it should be supplemented by a qualifier. See **Equity Net Cash Flows** and **Invested Capital Net Cash Flows.**

Net Present Value—the value, as of a specified date, of future cash inflows less all cash outflows (including the cost of investment) calculated using an appropriate discount rate.

Net Tangible Asset Value—the value of the business enterprise's tangible assets (excluding excess assets and nonoperating assets) minus the value of its liabilities.

Nonoperating Assets—assets not necessary to ongoing operations of the business enterprise. {NOTE: In Canada, the term used is "Redundant Assets".}

Normalized Earnings—economic benefits adjusted for nonrecurring, non-economic, or other unusual items to eliminate anomalies and/or facilitate comparisons.

Normalized Financial Statements—financial statements adjusted for nonoperating assets and liabilities and/or for nonrecurring, noneconomic, or other unusual items to eliminate anomalies and/or facilitate comparisons.

Orderly Liquidation Value—liquidation value at which the asset or assets are sold over a reasonable period of time to maximize proceeds received.

Premise of Value—an assumption regarding the most likely set of transactional circumstances that may be applicable to the subject valuation; for example, going concern, liquidation.

Present Value—the value, as of a specified date, of future economic benefits and/or proceeds from sale, calculated using an appropriate discount rate.

Portfolio Discount—an amount or percentage deducted from the value of a business enterprise to reflect the fact that it owns dissimilar operations or assets that do not fit well together.

Price/Earnings Multiple—the price of a share of stock divided by its earnings per share.

Rate of Return—an amount of income (loss) and/or change in value realized or anticipated on an investment, expressed as a percentage of that investment.

Redundant Assets—see **Nonoperating Assets**.

Report Date—the date conclusions are transmitted to the client.

Replacement Cost New—the current cost of a similar new property having the nearest equivalent utility to the property being valued.

Reproduction Cost New—the current cost of an identical new property.

Required Rate of Return—the minimum rate of return acceptable by investors before they will commit money to an investment at a given level of risk.

Residual Value—the value as of the end of the discrete projection period in a discounted future earnings model.

Return on Equity—the amount, expressed as a percentage, earned on a company's common equity for a given period.

Return on Investment—See **Return on Invested Capital** and **Return on Equity**.

Return on Invested Capital—the amount, expressed as a percent-age, earned on a company's total capital for a given period.

Risk-Free Rate—the rate of return available in the market on an investment free of default risk.

Risk Premium—a rate of return added to a risk-free rate to reflect risk.

Rule of Thumb—a mathematical formula developed from the relationship between price and certain variables based on experience, observation, hearsay, or a combination of these; usually industry specific.

Special Interest Purchasers—acquirers who believe they can enjoy post-acquisition economies of scale, synergies, or strategic advantages by combining the acquired business interest with their own.

Standard of Value—the identification of the type of value being utilized in a specific engagement; for example, fair market value, fair value, investment value.

Sustaining Capital Reinvestment—the periodic capital outlay required to maintain operations at existing levels, net of the tax shield available from such outlays.

Systematic Risk—the risk that is common to all risky securities and cannot be eliminated through diversification. The measure of systematic risk in stocks is the beta coefficient.

Tangible Assets—physical assets (such as cash, accounts receivable, inventory, property, plant and equipment, etc.).

Terminal Value—See **Residual Value.**

Transaction Method—See **Merger and Acquisition Method**.

Unlevered Beta—the beta reflecting a capital structure without debt.

Unsystematic Risk—the risk specific to an individual security that can be avoided through diversification.

Valuation—the act or process of determining the value of a business, business ownership interest, security, or intangible asset.

Valuation Approach—a general way of determining a value indication of a business, business ownership interest, security, or intangible asset using one or more valuation methods.

Valuation Date—the specific point in time as of which the valuator's opinion of value applies (also referred to as "Effective Date" or "Appraisal Date").

Valuation Method—within approaches, a specific way to determine value.

Valuation Procedure—the act, manner, and technique of performing the steps of an appraisal method.

Valuation Ratio—a fraction in which a value or price serves as the numerator and financial, operating, or physical data serve as the denominator.

Value to the Owner—see **Investment Value.**

Voting Control—de jure control of a business enterprise.

Weighted Average Cost of Capital (WACC)—the cost of capital (discount rate) determined by the weighted average, at market value, of the cost of all financing sources in the business enterprise's capital structure.

Index

I, J, K

W, X, Y, Z

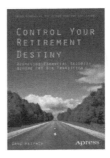